Oh, My Child, My Child: The Dilemma of Clergy Confronting Personal Grief

Rev. Dr. George F. DeFord

Praise for

Oh, My Child, My Child: The Dilemma of Clergy Confronting Personal Grief

The topics of grief and mourning are fundamental to life. This book clarifies the difference between the two. The author is at his best when he inserts stories from his personal experience. These are fresh and compelling related to the book's themes.

The impact of the book will be far-reaching. First, these are universal emotions and reactions to the universal realities of death, and loss. It is dear to all of us who have lost loved ones and can't imagine what it would be like to lose one's child.

This is an important work for clergy because we tend to focus upon those who are active in the church and less attention given to those who are disabled, elderly and otherwise out of sight. Therefore, it is important that we bring appropriate sensitivity and a knowledge-based behavior to situations of grief and mourning. This book will help us do that. Because it leads us to reflect upon similar stories from our own experiences, it is excellent, thought-provoking mediation.

An excellent—*for instance*—is of clergy's need for therapy, which has had a stigma attached to it previously, especially in the Black church world ... A case is made for clergy being in a therapy group with other clergy. Notable, is this author's quote, "We stuff it under our robes and go out."

DeFord skillfully weaves his expertise on the subject throughout the interviews.

Another very interesting reason why members of clergy don't reach out to other clergy members with their grief is, *I don't want to burden another clergyperson. They have their own struggles* ...

An important theological question is posed, "Do we believe that if we do good, no harm will come to us?"

—Rev. Dr. Delores Carpenter, Professor Emeritus at Howard University School of Divinity, Washington, D.C.

***

Rev. Dr. George DeFord has written an authentic, powerful, heartfelt, and vulnerable discussion of the multiple challenges clergy face after the death of a child. As Dr. DeFord shares his own suffering and the suffering of other clergy losses in these deeply honest narratives, the #1 challenge for clergy and clergy families is our own acknowledgment that we can benefit from seeking grief therapy after the death of our child. Well ... the death of a clergyperson's child is an experience that should move us to *Run, not walk, to therapy so we can be cared for!* What psychological, cultural, and spiritual barriers influence why clergy do not seek the professional care they deserve, especially after the death of a child? This book highlights honest challenges [internal, external, cultural, and ecological] and provides hope, encouragement, and recommendations.

I pray you will gift yourself with professional care so that we all heal in the way God desires for us and find meaning and hope in this world as we continue our bond with our loved child/dren beyond Earth.

—Deborah G. Haskins, Ph.D, LCPC, Board-Approved Supervisor, MAC, ICGC-II, CCGSO, CGT

***

I agree that this is an important area to look at. I was a pastoral psychotherapist for most of my ministry and worked with grief for almost all my clients. And clergy tends to not always care for themselves emotionally, so it is an important area. Having a clergyperson address this critical issue may help other clergy members consider the care they need after the loss of a loved one. And it may be helpful for congregations to understand more clearly what a pastor needs at such a time.

The interview with Dr. Haskins was very revealing and got to the heart of the issues around her own emotions, how she handled them, and her responses to those around her. Rev. DeFord's observation at the end of the interview was well written and summed up the interview well.

—Rev. Kathleen H. Kohl, RE, UMC, Pastoral psychotherapist at Pastoral Counseling & Care Ministries, Silver Spring, MD

***

Rev. Dr. George DeFord shares poignant and personal memories of his grief journey, following the tragic loss of his son in *Oh, My Child, My Child*. As ministers, we are equipped to offer encouragement, support and even counseling to our parishioners, but who do we, as ministers, turn to when we experience profound loss and grief? Rev. Dr. DeFord's moving account of his own grief and accounts shared by other clergy in the book, provide invaluable guidance for navigating the grief journey. His experience and advice resonate with clergy, regardless of where we are in our careers—seminarians, early career, or veteran. He asks questions we've probably all asked ourselves as pastors—'is it better to rely on faith when experiencing personal loss or seek counseling; will my members think less of me if I'm transparent about my grief, will I be perceived as hypocritical for espousing scriptures and promises of eternal life and joys of Heaven when I don't find comfort in any of this in my own grief?' This book is an excellent resource for self-help and self-care for pastors. It is a book to read now and put on the shelf for future reference and support.

—Rev. Dr. Eugene Matthews, Retired, District Superintendent, Baltimore West District, Baltimore-Washington Conference, The United Methodist Church

**

I really appreciated how he differentiates between grieving and mourning. I found this to be helpful and something that made me think.

—The Rev. Dr. F. Douglas Powe, Jr., Director of the Lewis Center for Church Leadership and the James C. Logan Professor of Evangelism, Wesley Theological Seminary, Washington, D.C.

***

Dr. DeFord has touched upon a nerve in his book that impacts clergy and laity alike. Unlike the interviewees, I have not lost a child; however, the pandemic introduced a season for various losses—personally and professionally. With loss comes grief and mourning, which take time to render itself benign. The stories shared were powerful and heart-wrenching.

Dr. DeFord did not gloss over the real hurt and pain each interviewee experienced, but he also provides a context for hope and healing—not forgetting. That's a gift to the distressed.

—The Rev. Dr. Evan D. Young, Executive Director Stakeholder Relationships, Discipleship Ministries, The United Methodist Church

###

G. Franklin DeFord, Publisher

Pomfret, MD 20675

Manufactured in the United States of America

Book Cover design: Visions That Transcend

Cataloging-in-Publication data is available from the Library of Congress.

ISBN: 979-8-218-22832-3

E-ISBN: 979-8-218-22833-0

Dedication

Clergypersons who struggle to confront their personal grief.

Acknowledgments

I thank my girlfriend and wife, who is one and the same, Lila A. DeFord, for her encouragement, prayers, and unyielding support for this venture. She prayed for this work, daily, to fulfill God's purposes.

I am deeply indebted to my colleagues and friends who took time from their busy schedules to offer personal accounts for inclusion in this guide and exploration into clergy grief. Moreover, there are no words to express the magnitude of my appreciation for each who shared their painful feelings and struggles as they recalled the occasions of personal grief and mourning, which still linger.

Representative of the group of suburban pastors are the Rev. Dr. Kay Albury and the Rev. Steven Tillet who both lost sons; two teenaged and adult children respectively. To these pastors, I am deeply appreciative.

Also with deep appreciation, I wish to thank Pastors Eloise Newman and Irvin E. Beverly who were examples of rural pastors who experienced the deaths of adult children; Pastor Newman, in particular, reported the contrasting responses from the churches where she was as a member and as pastor.

Rev. Dr. Sue Shorb-Sterling and Rev. Dorothea B. Stroman brought unique perspectives as members of extended kinship groups, i.e., grandmother and aunt, who felt the deep pain of grief along with the parents (of whom, one was clergy) of the children who died. To these two pastors, this author is especially grateful.

I am beholden to Dr. Deborah Haskins, widow of the late Rev. Dr. Bruce Haskins, and Rev. Dr. John Warren. Both respondents courageously and openly shared their experiences with violence resulting in the deaths of loved ones. Dr. Haskins suffered the murder of an adult child and pining death of her clergy spouse. While on the other hand, Dr. Warren received the tragic news of the murder of his grandchild and suicide of his adult child. Each individual revealed the manner in which they dealt with the heart-wrenching events and the responses of their churches. To this end, I am without sufficient words to express my gratitude for my colleagues volunteering to speak about their personal tragedies.

I thank Rev. Terri Coffiel who, in the midst of her personal sorrow, having lost her mother and years before, her husband, was able to initiate a resolution that is now Baltimore-Washington UMC Conference policy, regarding *Establishment of the BWC Clergy Bereavement Protocol and Policy*, effective July 1, 2023.

I thank the following giving persons, other relatives of clergy, willing to be interviewed: Gwendolyn Kent, Beverly McKenny, Beverly Johnson, Jocelyn Moore, Karleen Powell, and Gail Mason.

I am further indebted to Certified Lay Minister Cynthia Belt Gipson, who is the sister of Rev. Dorothea Stroman and the widow of the late Rev. Joseph Gipson.

I also thank Rev. Obie Wright, Jr., my former professor and friend, for his valuable critique that helped the trajectory of my summations as well as Rev. Dr. Rodney Thomas Smothers for his input.

I am indebted to my colleague, friend and high school chum, Rev. Dr. Emora T. Brannan, for his invaluable comments and recommendations, supporting the worthiness of my exploration into the least discussed subject of clergy confronting the personal dilemma of losing a child.

Finally, I am absolutely indebted to Mrs. Yvonne J. Medley, founder of the Life Journeys Writers Guild and writer coach-editor, who walked with me throughout this writing. Mrs. Medley's guidance has been of inestimable value. I shall always be deeply appreciative for her help.

Foreword

In this resource, Rev. Dr. George DeFord has given us an intimate look at grief from his first-hand experience as one who has experienced generational grief. His multiple views of grief as a son, father, friend, and pastor are illustrated with such a depth of intensity that, as a reader of these occurrences, one cannot help but experience the triggers that death and grief bring to all our lives.

DeFord's scholarship and his expertly researched biblical history of the customs and traditions of death and grief through biblical history, combined with cultural sensitivities and his clear-eye interpretation of grief from regular passages of sickness and death due to age, unexpected death through trauma and tragedy and death from the viewpoints of a pastor who has led his parishioners through the many seasons of death and dying.

His reflection on the need for professional counseling to navigate the lingering impact of grief upon our faith, our focus, and our future is an invitation to insist that we not attempt to undertake grief without a community of people, both trained and non-credentialed to accompany us through the stages of grief, grace, and gratitude.

Dr. DeFord's near-death experience as he lived through COVID-19 has somehow woven its impact into this insightful book. When you have personally knocked on death's door, it certainly informs your journey of death and grief. This book is a journal, textbook, grief manual, and inspiring biography of how to navigate grief and accept its lingering impact on our lives and reminds us that as we experience the inevitability of death, we should live as an informed witness that living with grief is not an event, it's a journey. Dr. DeFord has provided us with a transformational resource that gives us insight into our own destination with grief—clergy grief.

Rev. Dr. Rodney Thomas Smothers

Retired UMC Pastor & Leadership Coach

Contents

Introduction

Among the myriad ministerial responsibilities assigned to pastors is the assistance offered to their parishioners navigating through times of grief and mourning. Providing pastoral counseling to the bereaved is emotionally draining for the church's spiritual leader, especially after a series of funeral services. Moreover, during the following Sunday worship service, congregants expect the preacher to deliver a rousing sermon of hope and joy while overlooking the possible countertransference of the burden of grief from the previous funeral service(s) weighing heavily upon the pastor.

The matter of preaching while emotionally drained due to grief is exacerbated when the minister confronts the complex problem of dealing with a family member who died. Although the church may provide time off for a grieving period or give time to care for their family, there is still the expectation that the pastor will manage their grief and continue to care for the church members.

However, in my experience as a pastor, early on in my ministry, colleagues suppressed feelings of grief to continue with a persona of spiritual strength during times of personal emotional pain. Hence, I, too, *stuffed my feelings of grief inside my robe* and proceeded to carry out my ministry as if the deaths of my loved ones did not pain me or, more to the point, that God had given me the power to suppress my real feelings. Moreover, the eruptions of my moments of outward grief occurred in my private safe spaces. I believe some of my colleagues behaved the same as I did. Really? Didn't we have to protect our image as pastors who were the personification of spiritual strength, proving that God was our help and stability in our time of need?

Now in the autumn of my life and ministry, while grieving the loss of my adult son, Christopher, the preceding questions caused me to investigate the matter of pastors confronting their dilemma of the deaths of their child(ren) and how to manage the problem of grief healthily and spiritually—that's with or without the help of professional grief counselors or therapists. Also, my particular account of grief and pain is not unique such as shown in the narrative of King David, whose rebellious son Absalom was killed by the northern tribes; David's response to his son's death motivated the title of this deliberate exploration of *clergy grief* and my journey into the same: *Oh My Child, My Child, Clergy Confronting the Dilemma of Personal Grief* (2 Samuel 18:33). So, I dare to share the stories of pastors, a widow of a pastor, a grandparent who is clergy and an aunt who is clergy of her nephew who died of a terminal illness and the manner in which the sampling of clergy and relatives confronted their grief.

Two situations during the 1990s when two late colleagues of mine lost their adult sons due to illnesses left an indelible mark in my memory. The first occurred recently after my appointment to a congregation in Baltimore City in 1993. My late colleague and friend lost his son, a licentiate minister, in a Baptist church. My late friend's sister shared with me about her brother, a well-known Methodist preacher. Beverly J., daughter of a preacher, *a preacher's kid or P.K.* (friendly labels often affixed to the children of preachers), shared several episodes in her family pertaining to occasions of grief while a child and as a young adult. Beverly J. believed as a child that preachers were fearless and untouchable by the grief of ordinary people. On an occasion, while living in a parsonage, Beverly heard her father, a pastor, crying loudly in his home office. Outside her dad's office, she asked, "What's wrong, daddy?" Her father replied, "Nothing."

Not satisfied with her father's answer, she went to her mother, who confided, "Your daddy's father died." Because her father was a pastor, he would not dare to cry publicly.

Beverly J., as an adult, and her oldest sibling remembered the time that their father died. While the entire family openly grieved, she explained, her younger brother did not mourn in full view of other family members; instead, her young preacher-brother went to the chapel in the hospital where he could release his tears privately. Beverly J said, "I found him in the chapel. I embraced him and asked, 'Why did you leave us?'" Her brother responded, "My strength is in the Lord, and as a preacher, I should be consoling my family instead of showing my own grief."

The same preacher-brother, many years later, suffered the loss of his son, a young, licensed Baptist minister. Beverly suggested to her brokenhearted preacher-brother that he should seek grief counseling. His retort was: "I lean on the Lord!" He took her recommendation—to seek counseling for his grief—as utter faithlessness and ridiculousness, to his preferred—*take your burdens to the Lord and leave them there.*

The second situation centered upon another late colleague of mine whose son died of a serious illness. The pastor's son joined the congregation in the fall of 1995. In February 1996, the young man died due to his illness. The son's Celebration of Life service took place on a snowy Friday morning. Although there was a small attendance due to the inclement weather, worshipers came from as far away as Washington, D.C. Given the weather; I began the service early. My late colleague during the service burst out with a scream, and uncontrollable tears as the funeral director closed the casket.

Moreover, the deceased son's bereft preacher-father rose from his pew, approached the coffin on the catafalque, and wept inconsolably while placing both hands on the top of the casket. The funeral director and another family member subsequently assisted him back to his seat. The preacher cried throughout the entire service; he was a broken father, a pastor who wept openly in public.

The image of my late colleague in such an emotionally distraught way due to grief shattered my impression of a pastor who was expected to be spiritually strong and emotionally immune to the piercing sting of the death of a loved one, especially a child, even an adult child. How naïve of me!

I believe much can be learned from the laity concerning managing personal grief. Shauntia, a certified life coach and niece of my wife and me, married in August 2018 and lost her husband in April 2019 due to a horrific motorcycle accident. The following months of grief and mourning were shrouded in the dark clouds of depression and questions of theodicy as to why a good God allowed such a tragedy to happen to her after only a brief period of happiness with the love of her life.

Our niece sought help from her esteemed pastor, who encouraged her to pray and provided a lot of scriptures. While she appreciated what her minister offered, it was not sufficient. Shauntia opined that the minister neither knew nor appreciated the value of grief counseling. In addition, well-meaning church members gave such sentiments as *God don't put more on you than you can bear*, or *God knows best*. Feeling that she somehow fell out of God's grace because of her lack of faith, our niece became angry with God. There was the constant refrain in her mind: "...how could a God that loves me so much cause so much pain?" Because of no reasonable answer, she abandoned the spiritual disciplines of fasting, praying, and reading scriptures daily due to the fear of being condemned for her thoughts of anger, rage, and hopelessness.

A salvific moment happened when a minister, Shauntia knew, saw the visible toll grief was taking on her, such as hair loss, muscle spasms, and so much more. Grief was toxic. The minister said, "... the journey of grief is not going to be easy, and it feels like crap, I know. You will have good days, you will have bad days; it may take months, or it could take years before you begin to feel like yourself again, but you have to get some help." The preacher gave her the name and number of a faith-based grief counselor. Our niece began her journey of healing, for which she had prayed, and the process grew clearer to her, pertinent to the meaning of *faith without works is dead* (James 2: 14-22). She reaffirmed her faith in God, who is a healer and a restorer, and she witnessed that whoever must confront the problem of personal grief should seek therapy and pray. Give thanks to God for the counselors of faith that serve as God's divine light in the moments of darkness.

The Rev. Dr. Arnold Howard, pastor of Enon Baptist Church, Baltimore City, disclosed during the 1980s, how the former Provident Hospital provided auxiliary space for counseling and therapy services for clergy. The service was not openly publicized for the purpose of maintaining the strictest of confidentiality. To his understanding now, the said service no longer exists.

The Rev. Dr. Howard-John Wesley is the pastor of the internationally known and renowned two-hundred-year-old African American Alfred Street Baptist Church, Alexandria, Virginia. The said congregation consists of over twelve thousand-plus members, a corporate level congregation.

Pastor Wesley while teaching the CAYA (Come As You Are) Bible Study on July 3, 2013 disclosed his dilemma of handling the heart-wrenching loss of his father and the unhealthy manner in which he dealt with the grief. He sought subsequently grief therapy from a therapist who was Jewish. The pastor jokingly stated, "I chose her because she was not familiar with me as a pastor ... had I chose an African American counselor it may have seeped out into the community." In addition, he revealed that for a three-month period he was unable to effectively serve the congregation. Most of all, anger toward God set in—a matter of theodicy. In my research, I found that men tend to deal with grief in unhealthy ways such as a dependency on alcohol and drugs or meretricious relationships to soothe their grief. Sadly, this does not exclude clergy.

The Rev. Dr. Angelo V. Chatmon serves as the pastor of Pilgrim Journey Baptist Church in Richmond, Virginia. He also serves as director of University and Church Relations at Virginia Union University as well as University Pastor. Dr. Chatmon shared with me on Good Friday, April 7, 2023, after The Seven Last Words worship service at Westphalia Christian Community Church, Westphalia, MD, that he lost his son, Malachi, in 2017. He disclosed how he thinks of him often. Dr. Chatmon shared that while he did not receive formal grief counseling, he did receive informal counseling from certain clergy friends with whom he felt comfortable.

In view of the foregoing narratives, I attempted to present to members of the craft the experiences in my life, episodes of grief, and how I dealt with the difficult situations as a young adult, as a pastor, and as a father. Additionally, clerics and their relatives shared their encounters with the ever-present emotion of grief, which can be a furious monster that attacks and makes itself known at any time. It is the constant reminder of the painful occasion of a loved one being forcibly taken away even though the event faded in the distance of time yet reappeared in an instant with force. It is a steady reminder of our powerlessness.

At the risk of being severely critiqued by exegetes and biblical scholars, we clerics are not immune from life's experiences. The psalmist stated, "Many are the afflictions of the righteous, but the Lord rescues them from them all ..." (Psalm 34:19). So it is; some pastors encountered the death of a loved one as a solely bitter experience. Metaphorically, their pain could be described as the distasteful waters of Marah (Exodus 15:23). After a period of time, pastors sought help to manage their grief. Help from faith-based grief counselors or therapists does not relegate a minister to the category of faithlessness or a spiritual weakling. Instead, receiving professional help to aid in the rescue from the depressing dark pits of grief can keep a minister strong. It's like Ebedmelech, the Ethiopian eunuch at the top of the cistern with ropes of deliverance (Jeremiah 38:11–13).

Through interviews, biblical examples, and actual accounts, the following pages unveil the phenomenon and challenges of clergy grief, including my experience when I

8

was forced to *stuff my grief inside my robe*—forced to suffer in silence. Or as Christal Brown Heyward, author of *Processing Grief Through the Eyes of Faith,* said, "As we move through grief, we do not have to suppress our emotions and be strong all the time."

Grief counselors address the current existential issues affecting a client, while therapists, who deal with grief, focus on helping patients to discover and understand problems originating in their past, impacting their present attitudes and behavior.

Together let's come upon the best pathways through the dark valleys of grief to gain solace.

CHAPTER ONE

The Painful Memory

Earlier Episodes of Painful Memories

My earliest memory of grief was during my childhood. In 1950, a telephone call awakened my parents and the family. Mama said, "George (my father), Wayne died this morning. We are going to Isabell's (my aunt)." One of my aunts who lived several blocks away from us was the caller with the bad news.

My mother, as I recall scurried around getting her clothes on. I cried perhaps because my mom was going to leave me at home with my dad and sister, Brenda, or maybe I cried because my infant cousin died. I cannot remember how long I cried that early morning. The other events I recall were family members in a flurry of coming and going to my aunt's apartment home on Harlem Avenue. Other than that, much faded from my memory. One thing I remember is the sadness I felt as a child.

The next significant episode of grieving was in June 1968 when I returned home from two weeks of active duty for training while a naval reservist. It was an early afternoon on Sunday when I arrived at my apartment a call came from Lawrence, a boyhood friend and college classmate. "Ford, you won't believe this, man. I don't know how to tell you. Edmond got killed in Nam after being only there thirty days.

Man, I can't believe it." Lawrence told me that he called a number of times to let me know. It was a painful jolt. He went on to recap what our group of guys had been doing upon hearing of Edmond's death: drinking, crying, recalling things we did as Boy Scouts, and the parties we attended as teens. Lawrence also told me of the wake that was scheduled for early that Sunday evening. I told him that I'd be at the funeral home with the rest of the gang. At the conclusion of the call, I nervously hung up the telephone.

At the wake, the emotional chaotic atmosphere was like waves coming ashore. There was uncontrollable crying and screaming by young women and men. The parents of Edmond kept repeating among their sobbing, "He was a good son. Why did God allow this to happen? All these criminals out here. Why did God allow this to happen?" George (Buddy) who was a former U. S. Marine, returned from "Nam" in 1967 was comforted by his wife, Ann, as he sobbed without control. Ironically, Buddy died in February 2022. Our original group of close-knit boyhood friends dwindled down to only two: Jackie and me.

I went to the flag draped coffin on the catafalque. On Edmond's casket was his picture in his graduation uniform from basic training. Tears began to flow from my eyes; I could not stop them. It seemed as though I was swept up into the groundswell of emotions within the room with the rest of my friends. It was difficult for the officiant to close the public viewing service that humid Sunday evening.

The funeral service at Enon Baptist Church, our home church, was packed to capacity. I arrived late; the service was over. A sense of guilt always plagued me for not being at Edmond's funeral service on that very hot Monday in June 1968. However, it would not be until November 2006 when the United Methodist Men of Metropolitan United Methodist Church where I served as senior pastor that we journeyed to Washington, D.C. to visit Arlington Cemetery, and The Vietnam Wall. I went to the station where the directory listed the names and locations of the deceased. With a tissue paper and pencil, I shaded his name on the paper. As I did that, I felt sadness that I had not experienced in years. In that private moment, I shed tears again. Even as I write this, I still feel some sorrow in my heart.

I still have joyful memories of we guys as teenagers. Buddy, Edmond, and I walking on Edmondson Avenue to and from Enon Baptist Church to attend Boy Scout meetings, Choir rehearsals, Junior Ushers and Youth Fellowship meetings. While walking what was affectionally referred to as *The Avenue*, we excitedly talked of the girls that made our teenage hearts throb, the immature aspirations of dating the girls, and laughing at the saints that got *happy* [especially a certain woman on the Gospel Choir who walked as she sang her solo] during worship services. I have mixed feelings of happiness and sadness as I look back on those days.

The next major episode of grief in my life was the death of my Aunt Annabelle (Nonnie) who was the grand matriarch of the maternal side of the family. Aunt Nonnie suddenly passed in the fall of 1973. She allowed me to stay with her and Aunt Bertha (a.k.a. Bert) during my college years at Morgan State (College) University where I commuted. Part of the agreement with staying with my aunts was doing the chores around the house and helping them with some of the heavy work.

Married with and one year old son, Christopher, and as a commuter federal government employee in Washington, D.C., I was about to leave for work when I received an early morning call from my mother.

She said tearfully, "...Annabelle died this morning!"

The call jolted me. My eyes instantly watered and I became somewhat speechless. I barely got the words out of my mouth, "Oh no! I'll be right there!"

Jean, my former wife, asked, "What's wrong?"

I replied, "Nonnie died this morning. I'm going there!" I called my office to speak to my supervisor who expressed his condolences and granted me leave.

At my aunt's home, family members gathered. Earl, my cousin and my aunt's only son, was very distraught. My cousin always impressed me as a fearless no-nonsense, World War II veteran Army sergeant, now a bundle of tears. Several of my aunts and my mother were comforting Earl, who could easily be mistaken for a professional football player. I tried to hold back my emotions without success. This was a very difficult moment for the family.

The funeral home dispatched staff members for the removal of my aunt's remains. In the meantime, the police filled out the death report. There were some outbursts of weeping as the staff removed Aunt Nonnie. My mother sobbed while I tried to remain her strong comforter and support during this stressful time. Meanwhile Aunt Bert, now the senior matriarch, was calm and presented a settling effect upon all present. Slowly, family members began drifting away as the early afternoon began. I took my heartbroken mother home where I stayed for a while then went home while still feeling the pain of my aunt's death.

A flurry of activities began in preparation for the Celebration of Life service. Periodically, during the week, I visited Aunt Bert who briefed me on the funeral services. The nephews were to be the pallbearers who would take our aunt to her final resting place.

The day of the funeral is somewhat of a blur. I recall being with my cousins and the gloves given to us as we carried the casket into the sanctuary and placed it on the church truck to roll it in position before the pulpit. During the service, I never focused on the eulogy the late Rev. Dr. Harold Carter, Sr. gave. There were periods of my sobbing while sitting with my cousins. At the conclusion of the service, we carried the casket from the church truck to the hearse. At the cemetery, we again carried the casket to the site of interment; we pallbearers stood behind the pastor as he performed the committal. While in ranks, I shed more tears.

After the service, perhaps perturbed at my display of emotion, my former wife said, "You need to stop crying."

All of us returned to the house where we ate, told jokes about my aunt, and the men had a few drinks on the third floor. Slowly, we all drifted away leaving my mother and Aunt Bert at the house. I felt so sad on my way home—feeling as though I was abandoning them, overwhelmed in bereavement.

January 9, 1990, presented an especially traumatic time in my life. This was the day, my mother, Inez, died. On January 8, 1990, I conducted a funeral service at St. Mark's UMC, in Laurel, MD where I served as senior pastor. Funeral services at this local church were large community events in which the entire church was filled to capacity, which meant about 200 mourners. However, on this particular occasion the decedent was the mother of three daughters and a number of grandchildren; the daughters were musical. Not only did they sing but they were emotive. Nevertheless, this service was unusually long and exhausting for me.

The repast filled the fellowship hall and lasted until about 3:30 p.m. Members of the hospitality committee prepared a take-home package and placed it in my office. Mrs. Eleanor M., chair of the Staff Parish Relations Committee, inquired about my mother. I told her that I was going to drive over to Baltimore to check on her, return to Laurel to get my belongings, and head home in Clinton. I left the church a few minutes before 4 p.m. with the intent to return no later than 6 p.m.

At my arrival to my parents' home in West Baltimore, a nurse from hospice explained that it would not be long before my mother would transition. What! I felt as if I were hit with a ton of bricks. Although my brother regularly gave me reports on my mother's condition, I did not realize the gravity of her illness.

The hospice nurse told us the medication that my mom needed to make her comfortable. As she prepared to leave, the nurse packed her medical accessories in the bag and gave what I thought was a standard expression of condolences in anticipation of my mother's demise. While my father appeared to be removed from the situation or just in a state of denial, I was trying to accept the reality that my mother was dying and how we would be as a family (anticipatory grief). The nurse gave me the prescription for pain-killer medication; immediately, I went to the pharmacy to get the prescription filled.

My younger brother served as my mother's caregiver. I stayed at the house with my brother and dad. My father periodically came in the room where my mother was in a state of pain, and Mama told my father during one of her more lucid moments, "George, I love you." Dad's facial expression was empty or expressionless. He just stared at mom and said, "I love you, Inette." Our parents were married for forty-nine years. My brother meanwhile went to his room, probably to shed some tears.

Eventually, I found myself morphing into my professional persona. I contacted the Red Cross that got in touch with my brother, Larry, who was an active-duty career military man. The agency made arrangements for Larry to get emergency leave and come home. We were a family beholding of six children. My other siblings came by the house during the evening. Dennis, a twin, came to see mom; he is a very private guy. After seeing mom, he went into the middle room where he cried. Dianna, Dennis' fraternal twin, came with her infant daughter, Tamara, for mom to see for a last time. Brenda, my sister next to me, visited and had prayer as a family. I also went to get my son, Christopher, to see his grandmother; she struggled to speak with him. Afterward, I took him back to his other grandmother's house. Returning to the house, I continued to give my present wife, Lila, updates.

The night would wear on as my siblings returned to their homes. I periodically went out to get coffee from the nearest 7-Eleven. I catnapped throughout the night until early morning and remained until early afternoon of January 9th. I updated Lila again and advised her that I was going home to get some rest. I left Baltimore, drove to Laurel, MD to the church to get my Bible, briefcase, preacher's packages, and headed home.

At home, I had to throw away the food that was left for me in the office at the church because the food had spoiled due to setting on my desk and being unrefrigerated overnight. I took a shower and went to bed. The next thing I recall wass Lila at home. Shortly, thereafter, my phone rang, Terry told me that our mother passed, my youngest brother said, "Hey Frank, Mama just died." I sensed he was fighting back the tears in addition to what I heard, the despair and numbness in his voice. I told him that we should be there in about an hour depending upon traffic. The ride from Clinton, MD to Baltimore City was a quiet trip without incident. Upon arrival at my parents' home, I saw familiar cars of family members. Inside, I could hear a little chatter, my father quiet, my older cousin Earl, now a deacon, giving words of comfort to some of my siblings. We exchanged greetings and finally I headed upstairs where my mother's body lay in the front bedroom. She seemed to be sleeping.

I assumed my pastoral persona. I did not cry. Immediately, I began to direct family members to gather around the bed, hold hands, and I began to read from the Pastor's Book of Worship, Pocket Edition. I read the ritual pertinent to immediately following death. I was so mechanical throughout this time. After the prayer, representatives from March's Funeral Home rang the doorbell. They entered and came upstairs to the front bedroom and began the process of removing my mother's body. I directed the family to allow the representatives to do their job. Once the men brought my mother's body from the second floor to the first and exited the front door, I heard my youngest sister loudly crying. Brenda and Lila comforted Dianna.

On the outside, some of the neighbors watched from their windows as the undertakers put mom's body in the back of the removal van. Once they left, several neighbors came to the door to express their condolences. I thanked them.

The following days were filled with preparing for my mother's Celebration of Life service. The service was at night at Enon Baptist Church. To my surprise, the hospitality committee of St. Mark's joined in with Enon's hospitality committee to help with the repast. Further, the choirs of St. Mark's joined with Enon's choirs that caused the entire choir loft to be filled to capacity. Colleagues from the Washington Central District came to participate in the Celebration of Life service for Inez DeFord. That night Enon's crowded pews included co-workers from each of our jobs. We had great support and felt that we put her away very nicely. I am sure Mama would have been pleased.

I spoke on behalf of the family. As a family, we felt the situation was surreal. Mama was dead! Yet, Rev. Howard gave a very fine eulogy and captured my mother's volunteerism with the hospitality committee over the years.

One thing that I remember throughout the initial experience, I did not cry. I don't know whether I was in a state of shock or was I trying to maintain my preacherly image. I just did not cry. Perhaps there was no time for tears—for the emotional release that I needed. I was busy with the preparation and coordination on behalf of my family. Is that what happened? How did others take my tearless reactions and emotion? Why and how is it that people react differently, especially clergy? I was a basket of tears when my friend, Edmond, died, why wasn't I the same when my mother died?

Grief does come. It was either during the last part of January or early February, I was in my office adjacent to our recreation area in the basement. It was as if a ton of bricks fell upon me. I began crying inconsolably. I could not stop. I never felt so powerless and weak as I did in that moment. I was alone. I wanted my mother to embrace and hold me as she did when I was a child and sick. But what I did was become overly engaged in work to avoid showing my wrenching pain and sorrow for losing my mother. I immersed myself to avoid facing the matter that Inez was no longer with us. Moreover, perhaps as a pastor, I thought either best, professional, or protective, not to reveal or express my grief openly. Apparently, I felt I needed to maintain a *stone-face* without showing my emotions. I stuffed my grief inside my robe. Are preachers to be immune from experiencing their grief and sorrow?

Later Episodes of Painful Memories

I expound on this segment as a recapitulation from an earlier book that focused on the celebration of life services in the African American churches in urban, suburban, and rural settings as an objective observer who could offer advice to the clergy community. However, not in my wildest imagination could I expect to become a participant in the vortices of my son's unexpected death, preparation for his

Celebration of Life service in the context of a multicultural setting, and in need, as a grieving pastor, of pastoral support during our families' mourning.

Like David who pleaded with God for his sick child to be healed (2 Samuel 12:15b-23), so we as a family prayed for Christopher's healing, a previous recipient of a kidney transplant and current dialysis patient. Now, he was critically ill in the University of Maryland Medical Center, Baltimore City. Christopher died May 28, 2018, 4:15 a.m. I was rudely awakened to a stark reality on several levels. Despite the many occasions I was with families at the deaths of their loved one and officiated their funerals, at the moment of my son's transition, I was not prepared or immune to the emotional pain of personal grief. My response was like King David upon hearing of the death of his son Absalom, "O my son Absalom, my son, my son!" (2 Samuel 18:33).

Karla F. Holloway in her book, titled *Passing On*, writes about the tragic death of her only son while she was writing her book. "My husband and I were too traumatized to make what is known in the industry as the 'first call'—the call to a mortician, notifying him of a death in the family ... It was not very long before we fell into the familiar business of a family who is bereaved; calling a pastor, speaking ourselves to the funeral director, arranging for our son's body to come home," says Holloway. I identify with Karla F. Holloway in my experience of Chris' death and the activities following.

The journey with my family and extended family brought two cultures together. Ellen, Chris' wife, and my daughter-in-law is White and my grandson, Christopher Junior, "CJ" is bi-racial. We walked this journey of Chris' sickness and eventual demise together as one family.

I recapitulate the events leading up to the time of Chris' transition. My son was hospitalized at the Northwest Medical Center, Randallstown, Maryland on Pentecost Sunday, May 20, 2018. He was transferred to the University of Maryland Medical Center Cardiac Unit, Baltimore City. After visiting with Chris on Sunday, May 27th, Lila, and I returned home in Charles County, Maryland. Ellen frantically called us late Sunday evening; she said, "They gave Chris only a 50-50 chance of making it to the morning!"

I responded, "We are on our way!" Truthfully, I was in no shape to drive because I felt as if I were hit in the gut by a football linebacker. Dante, my loving son by marriage, and Robin, his wife, drove Lila and I to the hospital in Baltimore. We arrived after midnight.

The next four hours were an emotional roller coaster. In the ICU Family waiting room, there was an uneasy silence periodically broken with sounds of slight mood lifters about Chris followed by sobbing. Also, in company with the family were members of the Color Guard. At my son's bedside, Ellen held his left hand, periodically crying and whispering to him that she loved him. Jean, my former wife, and mother of my son was very anxious, jittery and sobbing. For the next couple of hours as Brenda, the nurse, tended to the various electronic devices that provided data pertinent to Chris' body condition, heart rate, pulse, and oxygen level; she was quite compassionate toward us. Lila comforted Jean. At one point a member of the nursing staff requested that there be only two persons in the room at a time. Ellen, Jean, and Lila left while I remained.

Dannett, a friend of Ellen and Chris, who remained at his bedside, shortly after I left hurried into the waiting room where she informed us that we needed to come back right away. It would be only a matter of time due to his weakening condition, that Christopher would pass. With Jean, Ellen, Lila, and myself present, Ellen gave the nurse permission to turn off life support equipment. The three women left while I stayed at my son's bedside at 4 a.m. The nurse said, "It won't be long, sometimes it takes up to a half an hour. We don't know." Between 4:10 a.m. and 4:15 a.m., my son gasped slightly, he turned his head from the right side, gasped again, then gasped with a little more force, then slightly raised his head, and made a final gasp and his head gently rested back. He gave up his spirit.

What took place was agonal gasping; gasping respiration in dying patients. The gasping respiration indicates cardiac arrest; it may be one or two breaths before death results in terminal apnea.

There was no further movement. I felt so helpless. "Bless yah! Bless yah! Bless yah!" I cried out. "The Lord giveth; the Lord taketh away; blessed be the name of the Lord!" I muttered. Travia, our niece, began to say the Psalm 23 and others joined in.

The family gathered around the bed shortly after Brenda, the attending nurse, and other staff removed the breathing apparatus. Chris appeared only to be sleeping now. I began out of habit to read from my Pastor's Handbook, United Methodist Church Book of Worship section, *Immediately Following Death*. For the moment, I went into my pastoral role and nearly detached from the situation as I read the ritual. Ellen, Lila, and others left; I remained at the bedside with Jean who was overwrought with grief. I began to cry with her and said, "The child, God gave us on Saturday night, September 24, 1972, left us on the morning of Memorial Day, May 28, 2018. Chris' mom held my arm and urged me to leave so that the staff could care for the body of our child in preparation for the funeral staff to eventually receive him. The walk seemed so long from room six of ICU to the family waiting room. In that dimly lighted room other family members, Color Guard members and friends in various groups began embracing one another. From each group could be heard sough and much weeping. The reality set in, Chris just died. Our son was not alive! He's gone! It was the dark night of my soul!

We all slowly dispersed and went our different ways. Dante and Robin were so caring and concerned about us as we walked to the garage. They asked, "Are you okay, Rev?" The ride back to Charles County seemed forever and a blur.

The next days were filled with planning and preparation for the Celebration of Life service for Christopher.

Reverend Marlon Tilghman, Chris, Ellen and CJ's former pastor and my friend, was with us at Northwest Hospital and at the University of Maryland Medical Center. His presence was much appreciated as he offered prayers for our families and my pastor-friend stated he would provide the Celebration of Life program as his personal gift to the family. He would serve as the eulogist at the funeral service.

Christopher's death was a profound shock not only to the family but to the community at large, especially youths and young adults. As family, there were no words to adequately describe our emotions and feelings. The presence of Reverend Marlon Tilghman significantly helped Ellen and CJ; however, I, as the father and a retired pastor who officiated a number of funerals more than thirty-plus years, needed a pastor during my moment of being grief-stricken. I felt alone. I felt alone. In my head, I recited several scriptural passages: "...the Lord gave, and the Lord hath taken away; blessed be the name of the Lord." (Job 2:21d KJV); "Yea, though I walk through the valley of the shadow of death. I will fear no evil: for thou art with me; thy rod and thy staff they comfort me," (Psalm 23:4 KJV). Although my wife tried to comfort me, I was in emotional pain deep down inside of my soul.

Grieving the loss of my son, Chris, continued. I felt something was zapped out of me as my energy level was low throughout the summer into the fall. In November 2018, I received a call from Gail M. Frantically and incoherently, Gail told me that Rachel, her teenage daughter, stopped breathing and the paramedics were transporting her to the local hospital in LaPlata, MD. Without hesitation, I told her that I would meet the family at the hospital.

I met with the family in the emergency room. To say the least, Gail was distraught. I stayed with them until Mark, her brother who is a police officer, came in the room where the family and I were gathered. In his official voice, Mark announced that his niece could not be revived. There was an eruption of screaming among the family members.

Gail had to be helped as she screamed and yelled, "No, no, no!" As all entered the room where Rachel's lifeless body laid on the gurney. After almost an hour in the room, I felt my own grief crashing upon me. I called Perry Taylor, a certified lay minister, to come help me. Once he arrived, I began the service for *Immediately Following Death*. As I began the ritual, I could not contain my grief and began balling in front of my parishioners. I gave the book to Perry who completed the service. Rachel's death exacerbated my own grief. I broke down in tears. Perry placed his hand on my shoulder to console me. I felt that I lost another child! I felt that I could not handle this anymore!

Minister Perry Taylor Remembers

The passing of Rachel Thomas was one of the most tragically traumatizing events that I have experienced in my lifetime. This young lady had such a vibrant personality with an infectious smile that would light up rooms upon her entry. Her candor was so refreshing that you instantly knew she was going to be great at whatever she set her mind to do or become.

As I recall receiving the phone call informing me of her unexpected passing, my heart dropped to the floor in total disbelief that her young life had ended. If my memory serves me correctly, the call came from Mrs. Lila DeFord, who in her own right was shocked beyond belief. She informed me of Rachel's passing and the concern she had regarding her husband, Reverend George DeFord. She asked If l wouldn't mind going to the hospital to check on her husband and assist him as needed both with the care of the family and the needs of her husband.

Upon my arrival at the hospital and joining the Reverend and the family members gathered in that emergency room, my heart dropped again in disbelief of seeing young Rachel's lifeless body lying on the examining table draped with a blanket to the shoulders as if see was in a deep sleep.

The room was filled with family, those closest to her in the persons of her mother, grandparents, aunt, and uncle along with a few other close relatives. It was a very quiet setting with limited conversation as shock was being replaced with the reality that Rachel has passed on to eternity.

As I focused on the Rev., you could visibly see the stress of disbelief on his face and that his heart was heavy. As we chatted, I sensed a weakness in his voice, but outwardly he maintained his role of the family's Pastoral leader. When questioned about his current physical state and if he needed anything, he responded, "I'm okay." He then discussed the needed spiritual words of comfort and prayer for the family, maintaining all professionalism as a man of the cloth, but having glimpses of human brokenness and weakness which we all were feeling as a result of the current situation we found ourselves in. Once all the family members had arrived, Rev. DeFord led a prayer of comfort and collectively we prayed the *Our Father*.

As we departed, I could see the toll that the unexpected death of Rachel had taken on him, but he consistently said he was okay!

My Feelings in Retrospect

In retrospect, the experience of Christopher's illness and unexpected death continues to pain me. Understand, I am not ruling out the profound death of pain my daughter-in-law Ellen, who walked this journey with my son, and Christopher Junior, "C.J." who lost his dad, and Chris's Mother Jean, who lost her son, and Lila, who lost her son by marriage to me; but I want to be transparent to those accepting the call to ministry and to have the awareness that we too are not immune to the pain and suffering due to the illness and death of a loved one. The professional persona we wear will be ripped off in the moment of our personal trauma. Not that we do not trust in God, know, and rely upon God's Holy Scriptures, but moments come such as Jesus' weeping outside the tomb where His dear friend

Lazarus was entombed and decaying. Or like Mary, the Mother of our Lord, at the foot of the cross where she watches her son gasp for His last breath, we experience hurt and emotional pain and bewilderment. In the words of the late Henri Nouwen, we become the "wounded healer".

My initial response to Christopher's sudden hospitalization was that *he will pull through this because of the prayers offered up by our intercessory prayer team*, Thursday evening Bible Study and listing him among our sick members. In fact, the Word of God says, "Are any among you sick? They should call for the elders of the church and have them pray over them, anointing them with oil in the name of the Lord. The prayer of faith will save the sick and the Lord will raise them up ... pray for one another, so that you may be healed. The prayer of the righteous is powerful and effective," (James 5:14—16).

A few months ago, when Chris had an episode of sickness and hospitalization at Northwest Medical Center, he broke down and cried. He cried in the presence of Lila and me and said, "Dad, I am tired of being so sick." Lila held him until he stopped crying. Shortly after that moment, he composed himself. I assured him that we were praying for his healing and that God would provide the kidney he needed.

Fast-forwarding to Sunday evening May 27th when Ellen called, hysterically crying saying it was doubtful that Chris would survive to the morning, I felt such a jolt I never felt before. My best description is that of being hit in the backfield by a football player linebacker and the breath was knocked out of me! "I knew the boy was slipping away from me ..." I cried out to Lila who was weeping too. I went into our master bathroom where I simply uncontrollably cried like a child. I lost all sense of time.

Again, attempting to describe my feelings can be viewed through the lens of Holy Scriptures. At moments, I imagine myself like King David crying for healing of his child born of Bathsheba and him but dies. (2 Samuel 12:14—19) Also, I can identify with David crying out because of the death of Absalom, his son: "O my son Absalom, O Absalom, my son, my son!" (2 Samuel 19:1—8) Like Elijah, I feel like I am in a cave and despondent. (1 Kings 19:4—18) Perhaps, similar to Jeremiah, the prophet of the Old Testament, found himself depressed and hopeless in a muddy well. (Jeremiah 38:1—6) Our Lord mourned the death of His friend Lazarus although He was able to bring His dear friend back from the grave. (John 11:28—44) I can imagine the powerlessness, pain, and sorrow Mary experienced while seeing her son Jesus upon the cross. (John 19:25—30) I hurt deep down inside of my spirit.

Yet, because I selfishly considered my own feelings, I needed to step back. The prayers prayed, I believe, were answered. I say that because in view of my son's fatigue with being sick received his healing through death. It was interesting that the medical staff at Northwestern Medical Center and the University of Maryland Medical Center could not come up with a conclusive reason as to why or what was causing Chris' decline. Our son no longer needed the various apparatuses for dialysis or the associated medicines to help sustain him. In a manner of speaking, he was freed.

Kala Holloway said, "DuBois wrote of his son's passing as 'liberation' and that his child was 'not dead, but escaped; not bound, but free.'" Holloway does not agree with DuBois; however, I feel that there is a ministry in death that frees one from unreasonable suffering and a less than a reasonable quality of life. Let me be clear, I am not advocating for medical assisted suicide, but I believe a person should be allowed to transition naturally rather than maintained on life support in a vegetative state.

I suffered COVID-19 during April 2020; the ICU physician asked if I wanted to be resuscitated. I uttered a quick prayer and replied, "Yes." At that point in time, I believed that should I stop breathing and be revived I would have an acceptable quality of life without being on a life support system.

I had a Job-like moment (Job 38). It may have been the day after Chris' death; I was reflecting back on my late niece, Tamara, who died in an automobile accident in June 2006 and the question Dianna, her mother and my sister, asked, "Why did God allow this to happen?" I heard the still small voice in my spirit say, "Chris is my child. I lent him to you, Jean, and Lila, for a time to exercise parental responsibility. What right have you to question me because I have brought him back home to me?" My moment of acceptance came but the grief and sorrow because of my love for him did not abate.

It occurred to me that in each of the churches that I served over the years there were parents who buried their children. At St. Mark's UMC, Laurel, Maryland, there is Gordon and Ann Gibson who buried Cory, one of their twin boys. Tyrone and Patricia Mundell who buried their son Tyrone, (a.k.a. "Ty"). George and Gloria Still whose son George, I officiated his funeral. At Mount Zion, Baltimore City, Dianna, my sister buried Tamara, and William and Fronie Cunningham laid to rest their daughter Trina. In Washington, DC, I funeralized Dana, the daughter of the late Joan Askew. Charles and Joan Davis lost their son. Metropolitan UMC, Indian Head, Maryland had its share of parents burying children: Vincent and Delinda Cooke (former wife) celebrated the life of their daughter Shayna. James and Margie Holly buried their daughter Stephanie.

A parent burying a child is not limited to the church within my sphere of ministry. My classmate Arthur I. Brown shared with me after the funeral of my son Chris that he understood my pain because he lost a child, a twin, many years ago due to illness. Arthur confided there is not a day that goes by that he does not think about his deceased son. I concur with my classmate that the death of my son Christopher continues to be a painful memory.

Also, I was impacted by the presence of parents, who loss children, despite the piercing resurgence of their own pain, attended the wake and Celebration of Life service of Chris. In the words of my colleague, the Reverend Dr. Timothy West, "The called are not exempt from suffering ..."

The death of Rachel further amplified my need to get counseling to help me deal with my grief. Seeing the family members of Rachel caused me to feel ineffective as their pastor. This was very painful for me.

Closing Thoughts

The experience of my son's death ushered in an entire unaddressed aspect of Celebration of Life services, for me. While being primarily focused upon African influences upon African American funeral services in various settings, it did not occur to me the African influences syncretizing with churches comprised of multicultural, multiethnic, and intergenerational groups. Milford Mill United Methodist Church in suburban Baltimore County is a melting pot in which reflects the ideal of a United Methodist Church, in my opinion. Dr. Arthuree Wright opined, "a foreshadow of the beloved community."

I discovered during the journey of the Celebration of Life for Christopher George DeFord that as a pastor I am not immune to grief and sorrow of the death of a loved one, especially one's child. All the emotions expected to happen such as anger, bewilderment, denial, depression, hopelessness, pain, powerlessness, and sorrow, to name a few, surfaced. Yet, we as a family were not alone. Friends and colleagues came along side with us during the difficult time of our mourning. Reverend Dr. Rodney T. Smothers, friend and colleague, said, "George, there is grief, followed by grace and then gratitude. You are grieving now but it's God's grace that is helping you and your family through this.

One thing you can be glad about, Chris was genuinely loved, and he reached a population that we as a church struggle to get. He had his own ministry."

Another revelation is when the pastor grieves and mourns, his/her congregation grieves and mourns also. The church wants to help in any way it can. Telephone calls, cards, flowers, gift packages, and visits all contribute to express the care of the church. It was very evident to me when Smith Chapel UMC rented a thirty-two-passenger bus to journey from Southern Maryland to participate in worship at the Celebration of Life service for our son. Moreover, the members of the church travelled in the motorcade to the cemetery. After the interment, I thanked them for their sacrifice to be with the DeFord Family and their reply was, "We love you." What an affirmation to receive from the church! Dr. Alfonso Harrod was right, "You have to love the people and they will love you back, Brother George!"

Pastors are not exempt from the pains and sorrows of life. Pastors are wounded healers. It is God's grace that sustains us that we in turn can help others. The apostle Paul said, "Blessed be the God and Father of our Lord Jesus Christ, the Father of mercies and the God of all consolation, who consoles us in all our affliction, so that we may be able to console those who are in any affliction with the consolation with which we ourselves are consoled by God." (2 Corinthians 1:3, 4) My son's death is still a painful memory that I want to share with colleagues as a means of equipping them should they have a similar experience. Thanks be to God!

CHAPTER TWO

Grieving And Mourning In Biblical Narratives

Grieving and mourning have been misunderstood and used interchangeably. It would be helpful to show the difference between the said terms; simply put, grieving is an emotion while mourning is a behavior and activity. Grieving is an emotion that happens within a person that experiences a trauma such as the death of a loved one while the outward manifestation of the feeling is mourning. Crying, screaming, fainting, wearing dark clothes, and funeral services/rituals are examples of the elements of the mourning experience. Succinctly, grieving within a person triggers outwardly mourning.

A closer look at grief and grieving is presented in the seminal work by Elizabeth Kubler-Ross, M.D. and David Kessler, *On Grief and Grieving: Finding the Meaning of Grief Through the Five Stages of Loss.* The writers expound upon the stages as: denial, anger, bargaining, depression, and acceptance. A person is shocked at the death and does not really believe that their loved one has died. Typically, their denial is expressed as, "I can't believe she's dead." Anger, although a necessary part of the healing process, may be directed at God or oneself. It is healthy to be angry at the death of a loved one. I observed some years ago when a young man suddenly died; while his lifeless body rested on the gurney in the emergency room, his grief-stricken young wife in the midst of her sobbing periodically gently hit him on his left arm then affectionately rubbed him and said, "Why did you do this to me?"

The next stage, bargaining brings into play the *what ifs*. What if I had not done this, she would still be alive? God, let this be a dream and my loved one will still be with me. The attempt to negotiate with God to reverse the circumstances in order for the loved one to remain alive is this stage of bargaining.

Depression, according to Kubler-Ross and Kessler, "... is a way for nature to keep us protected by shutting down the nervous system so that we can adapt to something we feel we cannot handle." Further, the authors assert, "A mourner should be allowed to experience his sorrow, and he will be grateful for those who can sit with him without telling him not to be sad. A mourner may be in the midst of life and yet not a participant in all the activities considered living: unable to get out of bed; tense, irritable, unable to concentrate; unable to care about anything." With such occurrences, it would be helpful to seek help from a physician.

Acceptance is the fifth stage. This stage is where a mourner acknowledges the reality of their loved one's death. Their absence is permanent. Moreover, acceptance is a process of recognizing the absence of a loved one.

My mother-in-law transitioned while a COVID-19 patient in April 2020. Prior to her being hospitalized, I recall her saying to my wife and I that she was tired and wanted to die.

However, we tried to encourage her not to want to die as there were many family members and friends that loved and needed her.

I was diagnosed with a COVID-19 infection and hospitalized several days after my mother-in-law's admission to the Intensive Care Unit (ICU). Ironically, Mother was in the room next to mine. It was late afternoon or early evening I remember hearing the code blue signal but did not learn until my return home six or seven weeks later that my mother-in-law died on April 10th in the late afternoon. I had difficulty accepting the fact that the grand matriarch of our family was gone. Even now, my wife and I periodically speak of Mother in the present tense, and when passing her room, I find myself looking expectantly to see her in the recliner looking at television programs or listening to CDs or writing notes to be mailed to family and friends.

We grow in accepting the fact that Mother Margaret is permanently absence from our family milieu but still have feelings of her still being with us. Acceptance is a process without a specific time frame of being achieved while on this journey of life.

Mourning as alluded to before is an outward expression of the internal emotion of grief. "It is the actions we take, the rituals and the customs," say authors Kubler-Ross and Kessler. As with grieving, it is a work in progress and has no specific time frame of reaching its conclusion. While in active ministry, I observed members that routinely came to the church's cemetery to visit their deceased loved ones' grave sites where they spent time alone. During the Celebration of Life services, some of the families were quite exhibitionistic in their tributes to the decedents. On an occasion, a plethora of flower arrangements, pictures on several bulletin boards, to use the expression, the family went, "over-the-top," in their tributes. Such outward display of expressions are means by which mourning is represented.

Mourning in the Old Testament in Hebrew refers to a range of emotive responses that include sadness, grief, lamenting, and weeping in connection to someone's death or a sorrowful or distressing event.

Also, mourning is expressing grief for the dead:

"The Hebrews expressed grief by tearing garments (2 Samuel 13:31; Joel 2:13), putting on sack cloths, and sprinkling dust or ashes on their heads (2 Samuel 15:32; Joel 1:8), by removing anything of an ornamental nature (2 Samuel 14:2; 19:24, Matthew 6:16-18). Professional mourners, mainly women, were sometimes hired (Jeremiah 9:17,18; Matthew 9:23; Acts 9:39). There was an extended period for mourning. They mourned for Aaron and Moses thirty days (Numbers 20:29; Deuteronomy 34:8) and for Saul seven days (1 Samuel 31:13).

***

Mourning was both private and public in which grief was expressed privately which there was a public enactment of lamentation. In the Old Testament, grief was to be exhibited publicly and loudly. Failure to do so was understood as disrespect for the dead, the bereaved family, the clan, the nation. The more significant social status of the deceased, the longer and elaborate funeral. Interestingly, I have seen this practice in our day.

In the New Testament, funeral rites are not described in detail contra to the Old Testament. However, Jewish funeral custom's included keening over the deceased by relatives, friends, and even professional keeners as a way of honoring the dead through displays of sorrow. Keening women began the lament in the home of the deceased and continued along the route of the funeral procession, with others from community joining in. For example, in the account of Jesus raising the son of the widow of Nain (Luke 7:11-17), apparently, there were women mourners in the crowd. Also, when Jesus was enroute to Calvary/Golgotha, there was a similar occurrence. The expression, *beating one's breast* is an example of grief, and *wailing* could be used of singing a funerary hymn or dirge. The women cited in Luke 23:27 were exercising anticipatory grief in view of our Lord's impending death.

In light of the above, grieving and mourning emphasis is upon the latter than the former. The outward conduct of grieving appears to be of more interest than the emotions related to death of a loved one.

One of the features less focused upon in the Old Testament is biblical characters that grieved and mourned the loss of their children. The account of Jacob (Israel) grieved and mourned the loss of his son, Joseph. His brothers lied about how he died. The patriarch characteristically mourned what he believed to be the violent death of his son, due to a wild animal attack. "Then Jacob tore his garments, and put sackcloth on his loins, and mourned his sons many days. All his sons and daughters sought to comfort him; but he refused to be comforted ..." says the text. The text continues with the following: "No, I shall go down to Sheol to my son, mourning." The concluding comment in the passage is: "Thus, his father bewailed him" (Genesis 37:29—36).

One can imagine the pain suffered by Jacob with the false information of his beloved son Joseph. The fraud perpetrated by Joseph's siblings can only be understood as in the context of a devious conspiracy without any sense of mercy. Moreover, the siblings joined in mourning with their father while knowing all along that it was a lie. One can only speculate how the brothers felt or was there a sense of guilt?

The First Passover was an epic moment not only in the history of the Israelites but also for the Egyptians. The death angel passed over at midnight and struck down all the first born of humans and animals in the land of Egypt. Pharaoh and all his officials arose at midnight and sent for Moses, as there was a loud cry in the land. Moses was ordered to evacuate the land immediately. The narrative is silent about mourning activities of Pharaoh for his son; however, presumably, the Egyptians followed their ritual for burying the royal child.

Pharaoh's firstborn more than likely was mummified as was the practice. The mummified body of the royal child was on a sledge that was drawn over the sand. Professional women mourners keened while covering themselves with dust. Further, personal effects of the child were carried to the place of his entombment; the corpse was usually transported by way of the Nile River. It is believed that the processional was one of grandeur. The final significant act of the ritual would be opening the mouth of the mummified corpse with an instrument known as a ritual adze, an arm-shaped tool (there were several types). Specifically, the type of adze used in this regard was called a pesesh-kef, which was made of stone and resembled a fish. This process signified that the mumification and revivification ritual was complete.

In view of the Egyptian families mourning the deaths of the firstborn sons, livestock, and the professional mourners, it was clearly understood ... "there was a loud cry in Egypt" (Exodus 12:30).

King David, the renowned biblical character, known for his psalms and military victories, suffered from sorrow and mourned the deaths of several sons, infant, and adults. The first child who died was the infant born through the adulterous relationship with Bathsheba, the wife of Uriah, a military officer. In an attempt to cover-up his illicit relationship in the pregnancy of Bathsheba, David conspired to have the soldier killed in the heat of battle. After Uriah's death, David brought his widow into his household, and she became his wife.

The prophet Nathan confronted David with his devious deed by way of a parable. What followed was the pinning sickness and death of the infant seven days after. In spite of the king's fasting and seeking God's mercy upon the situation, the child died, and David ceased from fasting, washed, anointed himself, worshiped, and stopped mourning. He went to console Bathsheba who conceived again and named the child Solomon (2 Samuel 12:1—25).

***

The next son, Amnon, under the pretense of being sick, wooed his half-sister, Tamar to his living quarters. He raped her. After the assault, Amnon threw her out of his living quarters because he despised her. Tamar in grief put ashes upon her head, tore the long robe that the royal virgin daughters wore; she went to her brother, Absalom who comforted her. After two years, Absalom exacted revenge upon Amnon by having him murdered by his servants. After the murder, Absalom fled to the king of Geshur.

Two full years later, Absalom returned to Jerusalem and did not meet with his father, King David. Notwithstanding, the son sort an audience with the king with whom he eventually met (2 Samuel 14:21—33).

The next tragic event in King David's life was the final rebellion of Absalom, who conducted an insurrection that caused the king to flee for his life. The king eventually regained control of the kingdom; he gave specific instructions to his military leaders not to kill his rebellious son. However, Joab, and ten of his armorbearers, disobeyed King David's orders and killed Absalom.

Two messengers, Ahimaaz and the Cushite, delivered the results of the battle and the status of the king's son. What followed was the expression of the king's profound grieving and mourning: "The king was deeply moved, and went up to the chamber over the gate, and wept: and as he went, he said, 'O my son Absalom, my son, my son Absalom! Would I had died instead of you, O Absalom, my son, my son!'" (2 Samuel 18:33).

***

We observe that the parent in grief is willing to take the place of the deceased rebellious son who was willing to kill the parent. The King's love for his treacherous son outweighed the transgression enacted against the father. Here, grief was proportional to the love one had for his child.

The extent of an Old Testament character exhibiting the ritual of mourning over her deceased sons is in the account of Rizpah, the concubine of Saul and five sons of Merab (a/k/a Michal) daughter of Saul. It was a case of retributive justice to satisfy Saul's action of pursuing the Gibeonites and killing them off on behalf of Israel and Judah.

A three-year famine occurred in the land. King David inquired of the Lord: "There is blood-guilt on Saul and on his house, because he put the Gibeonites to death." (2 Samuel 21:1) The Gibeonites wanted justice to which the king commanded that seven of Saul's children be handed over to the Gibeonites for execution on the mountain in Gibeon. The sons of Rizpah, Armoni and Merib-baal, and the sons of Michal were executed by impaling.

Rizpah's expression of mourning was taking sackcloth and spreading it over a rock for herself from beginning of harvest until rain fell. The concubine prevented birds by day and wild animals by night to come and ravage the bodies (2 Samuel 21:10). When King David heard how Rizpah mourned and protected the remains of the seven, he ordered that the bones of Saul and Jonathan be retrieved from Gilboa and brought to the tomb of Kish in the land of Benjamin in Zela. The bones of Saul and Jonathan and the seven sons were entombed together (2 Samuel 21:11—13).

The nameless and silent wife of King Jeroboam according to other ancient texts was an Egyptian princess named, Ano. Her husband directed her to disguise herself as another woman and seek information from the blind prophet Ahijah. Upon coming into his presence, Ahijah greeted her as the wife of Jeroboam. He had no good news for the king's wife as he prophesized doom to the kingdom. Moreover, she learned from the prophet that upon her return home, her child would die. The wife left the prophet and went home in Tirzah. As she entered the house, the child died. The text succinctly closed with the following: "...the child died. All Israel buried him and mourned for him, according to the word of the Lord" (1 Kings 14:1—18).

The biblical narrative about Job in the Old Testament (Hebrew Bible) was a didactic story. Job was a righteous man, blessed by God with prosperity evidenced by a large family, material wealth and social status and power in the community. However, he became the subject of a dialogue between God and Satan who served as the accuser of humankind before God. Satan acknowledged that God protected Job, but argued without the Divine protection, Job would curse God before God's face. God gave Satan permission to test Job through a series of tests with the stipulation that he would not take the patriarch's life.

Job is a poignant example of a parent's knee-jerk reaction to a tragic loss of his young adult children. The patriarch made daily intercessions on behalf of his offspring; in case they sinned against God. Perhaps Job felt he could gain immunity because of his righteousness.

***

Professor Carol A. Newsom, an American biblical scholar says, "... a theology that contains the unspoken assumption of a contract with God: God is bound to protect me [and my children] from tragedy because I have been good or simply because I belong to God. Such a *little faith* will not sustain a person in crises..."

***

47

Succinctly, Job daily bargained with God. Yet he was not immune to the unthinkable pain and sorrow that resulted from a destructive windstorm, causing the death of his children.

The narrative described the customary gestures of mourning by tearing his robe and shaving his head. His behavior was illustrated in other biblical characters who practiced similar mourning rituals. For example, Jacob upon hearing of the presumed fatality of his son, Joseph, tore his garments and put sackcloth on his loins and mourned for his son many days (Genesis 37:34).

Joshua, the successor of Moses, along with elders, fell prostrate before the Ark of the Lord because of the shameful retreat of three thousand Israelites before the men of Ai. Joshua and the elders stayed until evening and put dust on their head (Joshua 7:6)—Eliphaz the Temanite, Bildad the Shuhite, and Zophar to the Naamathite.

The compassionate friends came to Job with the intent to mourn with him for seven days and nights. Essentially, the three friends exercised a ministry of presence, none of them spoke. However, after Job lamented his situation in chapter three of the Book of Job, the ministry of presence transitioned from compassion and empathy to a time of indictment based upon presumed sins and unrighteous behavior by the patriarch.

A similar scenario happens today in our world. Friends come with a notion to be compassionate and empathic; yet they make the blundering mistake of saying the wrong thing to the bereaved. I have heard: *They're in a better place now* or *God saw a beautiful flower, so He picked it to decorate His garden in Heaven.* Such comments, intended to be well-meaning and comforting simply exacerbate the grief and pain due to the death of a loved one.

Job's friend intended to challenge him to do some introspection for the purpose of discovering why these calamities came upon him. Yet, the friends were wrong because they said the wrong things, later in the narrative they repented of their errors.

The Book of Job, though some view it as a folktale, provides a cogent illustration of a parent suffering pain and sorrow due to the loss of his or her children and the outer responses one might receive to such personal grief.

Personal grief, thus far, is the focal point in the biblical narratives. Careful reading of the Hebrew Scriptures, however, also addresses communal grief. The book of Lamentations, consisting of five short chapters, shed light upon the community in corporate grief. Although its authorship is in question among biblical scholars, Jeremiah is the credited author. The book of Lamentations is a part of a collection of five scrolls, Megilloth. In an acrostic fashion, Lamentations captured the enormity of grief and the raw emotions that coursed through the defeated people of Jerusalem, where the Neo-Babylonians invaded in 586 B.C.E.

Moreover, in the second chapter of Lamentations, a speaker metaphorically described Jerusalem as the daughter of Zion; also, the speaker gave a graphic description of a widow who grieved the loss of a number of her children due to starvation (vv. 11—12). Because of its corporate sinfulness, the daughter of Zion suffered the judgment of God through the instrumentality of Neo-Babylonian regime.

***

The Old Testament presents episodes of grieving and mourning that point out how the biblical characters dealt with God's judgments and mercies within the context of their particular life situations.

The New Testament accounts, especially in the Gospels, give glimpses of our Lord ministering to the grief and mourning activities of persons touched by His ministry. There are several accounts that present a child, a young adult, and a friend of our Lord that center upon their deaths and revivals.

Perhaps Matthew, in his gospel account, made an oblique reference to Jesus possibly mourning the death of His first cousin, John the Baptist. Jesus, upon hearing of the excruciating and horrific death, the decapitation of John at Machaerus, left the western side of the Sea of Galilee (Jewish side) to the eastern side (Gentile territory) in a boat to go to a deserted place by himself. Upon arriving ashore, he saw a great crowd that needed His healing ministry (Matthew. 14: 13-14). Initially, had He gone there to mourn, but was distracted by the needs of the people?

I contend Jesus needed time to grieve and mourn the loss of His cousin, John. Although the Bible is silent about what He felt; yet the circumstantial evidence points to the need for solitude and prayer to deal with His own sorrow. What relative would not want to grieve and mourn the loss of an extended family member? So, it could have been with Jesus. Similarly, most pastors who suffered personal grief feel compelled to respond to the needs of their congregation without sufficient time to grieve and mourn their loss while not having needed rest in a quiet space.

The familiar story of the widow of Nain whose son died is an example of Jesus' compassion upon the widow because without her son there would be no means of support for her in the community. Accompanying her according to the text was a large crowd, presumably among whom were professional mourners. Jesus said to the mother, "Do not weep." He approached the brier, command the bearers to stop, and through His divine power, He directs the deceased young man to rise from the clutches of death. The young man responded by sitting up and beginning to speak. Our Lord gave him back to his mother (Luke 7:11—16).

In another episode, Jesus restored a child from death. He was notified of the death of Jairus' daughter. At his arrival at the synagogue leader's house, there was weeping and wailing by all present. Jesus told them that the daughter was not dead, but the response of the crowd was disbelief. In like manner as He spoke to the widow's son, Jesus said, "Child, get up!" (Luke 8:54). The child's spirit returned, at once, and she got up. He then instructed them to give her something to eat.

A well-known account of our Lord's grieving and mourning the death of His friend Lazarus. The text records our Lord escaping from the vicinity of Jerusalem to across the Jordan to a place where John the Baptist baptized early. The message was brought to Him of Lazarus' death, but He delayed going to the home of His friend. However, when He did arrive, Mary and Martha, sisters of Lazarus, were saddened and Mary felt had Jesus been there, their brother would not have died. Mary appeared to be the more emotional sibling.

John described our Lord's emotional response. Jesus wept. He was deeply disturbed when He came to the tomb. Jesus gave the order to take away the stone to the entrance of the tomb. Martha, however, felt by this time, four days later, the body of her deceased brother was smelling due to decomposition. (It was the Jewish belief that after four days of death the spirit would no longer linger with the body.) However, our Lord demonstrates that not only does He have power over death but also, He is the resurrection and the life. Hence, He was able to call His deceased friend, Lazarus, back from death. Only the physical wrapping of the grave clothes kept him bound (John 11:1—44).

Another important event took place in the home of Lazarus, Mary and Martha. It was a situation of anticipatory grief. Mary took a pound of costly perfume made of nard and anointed Jesus' feet. Judas Iscariot chided for Mary doing the anointing and that the perfume could be sold for a certain amount of money, Jesus replied to leave her alone as she was preparing His body for burial. Mary was anticipating Jesus' death and expressing her grieving within and her mourning outside in the presence of those gathered.

The crucifixion not only was part of the redemptive experience for the believers receiving the gift of salvation and eternal life but a time of sorrow for God the Father. The concept of darkness is understood as a time of judgment. Yet, I view the darkness that was over the land from the sixth to the ninth hour as an expression of God's grieving and mourning the death of God's only begotten son. The prophet Amos said, "On that day, says the Lord God, I would make the sun go down at noon, and darken the earth in broad daylight. I will turn your feasts into mourning, and all yours into lamentation; I will bring sackcloth on all loins, and baldness on every head: I will make it like mourning for an only son, and the end of it like a bitter day" (Amos 8:9—10).

The ancient prophet addressed the judgment that was to come upon Israel, on the day of our Lord's crucifixion. God brought judgment against the nation meanwhile expressing God's grieving and mourning the death of his only begotten son.

CHAPTER THREE

Two Suburban Pastors' Experiences

with Loss of Children

Several suburban pastors, male and female, lost their children. After the deaths of their young and adult children, while one declined to seek grief counseling, the other sought and continues in grief counseling. A clergy woman describes the loss of her granddaughter and its impact on her daughter, son-in-law, and herself.

Rev. Stephen Tillet's Church Setting

Broadneck Community is the site of Anne Arundel County's first European settlement in 1649. The first settlers were Puritan from Virginia who were invited by Maryland's proprietary rulers Cecilius Calvert, 2nd Baron Baltimore to settle on the western shore of the Chesapeake Bay.

Asbury Broadneck UMC is an historical African American church. It is reported that the church began before 1851 when enslaved men of African descent started meeting at a place called *Old School House Hill* to praise God in their own way. This was before a church house. But the first church was built only yards from the original meeting location on St. Margaret's Road, which is now meeting House Lane South of Route 50 east of Annapolis, MD.

The setting of Asbury Broadneck United Methodist Church, Annapolis, Maryland, is a community that is experiencing gentrification. The once predominantly African American community is changing to middle to upper income with mainly White occupants.

MY INTERVIEW WITH THE REV. STEPHEN TILLET

George: I am Reverend George DeFord interviewing Reverend Stephen (a.k.a. Steve) Tillet on October 18, 2021, at 10:52 a.m.

Reverend Tillet, do you agree to this interview and share information concerning the matter of personal grief and mourning?

Steve: I do.

George: This project is devoted to recording conversations with clergy colleagues who have suffered death of a loved one, in particular, a child, young adult or adult. The intent is to gather information to write a book pertinent to clergy and their grief regarding the loss of their child or children. This interview consists of two parts, one being the initial grief and mourning responses. The second part concerns the lingering effects from the death of a loved one. Steve, describe the congregation you were serving at the time of the death of your son.

Steve: My son passed on the 11th of September 2020 while I was serving Asbury Broadneck United Methodist Church in Annapolis, Maryland. I had been serving as pastor [of the church] at that point for sixteen years.

The setting of the church is suburban although previously a rural community.

The average worship attendance was probably between 140 to 150 worshipers, pre-COVID. We've been of course, virtual for the last nineteen months.

George: Have you been able to assess your virtual attendance?

Steve: It's hard to say because some will be on Zoom, of course you'll have families on Zoom—one square, like the Hollywood Squares [television game show]. Then of course, there are people who watch Facebook. Over one hundred, and then some people tune in later and watch. So, it's hard to say.

George: What was your knee-jerk reaction to the news of your child's death and how did the family respond?

Steve: [It was] Unlike when you just receive the news straight out, and it's absolute shock. I had just by virtue of the way communication was trickling out, an opportunity to wrap my mind around the possibility of bad news a little bit. What had happened was I received a phone call from a number I did not recognize and so I didn't answer it. As you know now even if we have cell phones, telemarketers can still reach us and annoy us.

Then when I saw a number, and then they left no message ... see that's the other thing. When I saw 410313, I said, 'Okay, that's the Howard County Government number. Maybe that's the police.' Of course, Andrew was living in Columbia, Maryland at the time. Then someone left a message saying that they were officer so-and-so from Howard County and if I can give them a call.

People don't leave you a message and say, 'We're just calling to tell you that your loved one is dead.' You get to brace yourself a little bit. When I finally spoke to them, because I called them back then and he said, 'We usually don't give news in this format.' All of this is sort of a precursor, so I'm getting it in advance. Those five words— those six words—five, 'We regret to inform you ...,' I was in the driveway at my house, and just went down on my knees—and he's gone. They were not able to tell me a whole lot of detail. He had gone into another person's apartment in the building he lived, and he collapsed.

I subsequently came to find out that he had gone up there to ... he had, I think, gone downstairs to his apartment to get his laptop because he was a musician. He was working on some beats and other things, and I guess he was taking it up there for them to hear it. He collapsed and I think they tried to administer first aid and then they called 911 and they came but he had expired. I came in the house, and I told my wife what was going on, just that I'd had these calls, nobody left a message and then I thought it was Howard County and I was going on. Then I came back in, and I said, 'He's gone.'

58

They had not been able to reach his mother because she wasn't answering her phone either. I think they tried to call her early in the morning. They started trying to call me at seven something, but again they didn't leave a message. I don't know if the first call was from the 313 number, or from an officer's cell phone, but in any case, no messages Then I'm like, 'Oh my goodness, oh my God, my son is gone and now I have to communicate this to his mother', my ex-wife.

My thought was I don't want to call her and give her this news and for her to be at the house alone, so I called her sister who lives in Prince George's County also and told her so she could get over there to her sister and let her know what was going on. At least then, I knew she would be with somebody that she loved, somebody that loved her at a time when you're getting the worst news that any parent gets.

She did not appreciate that, because she was like, 'Well you should have just called me,' and I'm like, 'You don't want to give somebody that kind of news over the phone especially, and I didn't want you to get it alone.' But as the ex-spouse, you are wrong no matter what you do. The time of preparing for her service and whatnot, and even the day of the service would be a time where I was taking a lot of incoming. I just chose to not respond in kind because in my mind it served no point.

So, she found out. Then she said she would call our daughter in North Carolina, which she did, and told her. About a week later they had a memorial service that I attended in Prince George's County. Then I had one the next day also at West River. Of course, we wanted it to be outside and people could be socially distanced and whatnot, so that was that.

George: Was his death due to prolonged illness?

Steve: No.

George: Was his death unforeseen?

Steve: Yes. It was not due to violence. He was thirty-four at the time of his passing. Way too young. My age, that was 2020, I was sixty. His mom was sixty also.

George: Was he buried or cremated?

Steve: Cremated, and his ashes are here at my office. His mom or sister were going to get an urn, and then when they get an urn, the funeral home with which I've interacted a lot over the course of the last eighteen years of ministry in Annapolis, they received the body. [They] Allowed his mom and sister, and I don't know if anybody else was with them, but I know his mom and sister came for a final viewing. I was not going to go, and then I actually got a call from our Bishop, and we were just talking about it. It was a pastoral call.

One of my duty stations in the Air Force was the Air Force Court Mortuary at Dover Air Force Base. Anytime you hear of bad news overseas it comes to Dover [Delaware], so I've seen folks come in there in all manner of condition and whatever. Just having been a pastor for the last thirty years, and living life for the last sixty years, you've seen a lot of people deceased and in caskets and whatnot. I was like, 'I don't feel like I need to do that.'

[The Bishop] says, 'Forgive me, but I'm going to push you little bit. I want you to think about that a little bit more because you don't want to make a decision that you can't undo, that you can't take back.' I thought about it, and I said, 'Okay, she was right,' and so I went to the funeral home. They had him in the little side room that you can come and view your unprepared loved one. I sat there a while, talked to him a little bit. I told him, 'So this is the first time I will get to speak to you, in recent years, where you don't interrupt.' Then he was cremated.

Eventually, they will get the urn, and then I'll try and coordinate getting the cremains back to the funeral home so that they can put them in the urn because that's not anything that a family should have to do.

George: What was the reaction from your congregation at this time?

Steve: Their reaction was perfect. It was very measured. Clearly, they were shocked, they were deeply saddened, but they gave us time. The first couple of days I was like, 'I don't really feel like people.' You don't feel like seeing a lot of people or having a lot of conversation.

They gave us a couple of days. Then when we let them know that we were ready, they came by. Even then it was very measured in the way it was done. Nobody came by for an extensive conversation or visit. They literally came by, and they would usually bring food, whatever gifts they had to bring. They'd hug your neck and get back in the car and go. Of course, that's September 2020, so everybody is still masked, and no one is vaccinated, so everyone needed to keep distance. We would meet in the driveway. They would bring what they brought.

That following Sunday, if my memory is correct, we had the service out at West River.

I shared the information with the three other congregations that I had served, all of them were represented because they had known Drew. [Steve names the congregations.] He had friends and stayed connected to them, although some of the people he was closest to had actually predeceased him, unfortunately.

Then some colleagues came and whatnot. I did not do anything other than to remember that I had almost forgotten to invite ..., because the DS [District Superintendent, UMC] came. I'd almost forgotten to acknowledge her, or have her come make remarks, and so I got up to do that. There was a point when I was going to say something, and I couldn't. It was a really good service. Not real churchy, because he wasn't churchy, but it was a good service.

One of our colleagues who I've been—she calls me Chaplain Big Brother because I wander into the military as a chaplain, and she is still there. She was promoted to lieutenant colonel this year. She is a triple threat, she can sing, play, and preach, so she played and sung. She gave some words of comfort. She gave something he would have called the eulogy there. Whatever that would have been. Then a couple of other people. Then a representative from each congregation and family member and whatnot. That's much that.

George: I think my niece was there.

Steve: She probably was. I don't remember. She probably was, because sometimes these details will sometimes escape you. It's just a blur, you know?

George: I understand.

Steve: Yes, I know you do.

George: Did the church give you any formal time off?

Steve: Yes, they told me to take as much time as I needed, and the Bishop said the same. I was gone until the beginning of November. One of my lay servants was like, 'You'll be coming back beginning of the year?' I said, 'No, it probably won't be that long, because there's a point where you just can't sit around, and not have a distraction. Work and just the things that you do, even if you're not doing it full thrusters, you are at least doing it.' That was at the beginning, the first Sunday in November, I went back.

George: Have you taken advantage of grief counseling?

Steve: One of my friends needed grief counseling, and he went. It was a blessing to him, and he called me up. 'Steve, take this name, take this number. You need to call him,' and I did. Reverend has been a real blessing to me for the past year or so.

He is out of First Baptist Church of Glenarden. He's on their ministerial team and that's his portfolio, is counseling and especially, I guess, grief counseling. It has been helpful.

George: Did you receive recommendations from the conference through the DS or the Bishop to seek grief counseling?

Steve: I didn't get any recommendations through the conference for that. Let me not misspeak; I don't remember. It certainly would have made sense for them to say, 'If you need counseling, we've got it,' but I just don't remember, because I did not avail myself to it at that time. Then as I said, [my friend] reached out to me and just insisted, 'Basically you're going to call him. You need this, even if you may not think you do, you need it. You're going to him,' and I did.

George: Did you find counseling helpful?

Steve: I did. I still do. We're still talking every week for the most part.

George: Have you recommended grief counseling to bereaved families of your congregation?

Steve: Oh, absolutely, absolutely!

George: Have you recommended clergy who suffered the loss of loved ones to participate in grief counseling only for clergy?

Steve: I have not. I may ask sometime. 'Are you getting some [help] because physician, heal thyself, don't work.' Put down the scalpel, call someone else. I may ask that question, or nudge a little bit, but not a whole lot. BUT what I will do is listen. [Here, Pastor Steve cites several colleagues who lost a wife, an adult child, and a grandchild, and the circumstances leading up to the deaths of each.]

George: It has been a year and a month since the passing of Drew?

Steve: Yes, it has.

You asked about feelings as we prepared for the funeral services. [My daughter and former wife] were preparing the first one and my relatives came, cousins and whatnot. And I had a cousin, I don't know where he fits on the spectrum, because, let me see, his grandmother and my mother are first cousins. Whatever that makes us, third or fourth cousins, but you couldn't tell us anything. We might as well be first cousins born on the same day, we're close. He and his wife flew in from Denver just to be with us. He's like, 'You ain't driving nowhere I got it.' I just got in his rented car, and he took me wherever I needed to go.

They were there at the service rooms and [my daughter] and their friends and family organized on Saturday and then down at West River with us on Sunday. Then afterward, people came over here. We actually were coming back up from West River. I was like 'You all like seafood? How many of you like creamy crab soup?' We stopped by Cantler's and got a whole bunch of food and came back here and sat down.

Which of course, that was a gift because that September 2020, you've been on shutdown. You haven't been around anybody, nobody has been around you but at that moment, we did it, and his family was right on point as well.

For that preparation, I was pulling together a lot of pictures for his program. Pictures from his life from birth all the way to—and I guess pictures at each of the different congregations—and just his life. [I] Ordered the service [i.e., designed the service], what was going to happen when, who was doing what? Then I was not dumb enough [he laughs], smart enough not to be dumb and try to jump up and do stuff. Everybody handled their business.

George: Did you feel immune to such unforeseen or horrific events?

Steve: No, absolutely not. Absolutely not. You are well familiar with the expression, *shit happens*. Actually, one of my friends—we grew up as neighbors a few blocks away, and I dated his sister, and then he subsequently became one of my fraternity brothers and he was special forces in the Army, jumping out of planes and all—he said, 'That's not the whole expression ... Shit happens, and babies die,' and I was like damn, but that's the expression. You never feel immune. You try and keep people covered in prayer and hope for the best.

I think about [a colleague of ours] and his family. His son is just swimming, and he gets his feet stuck in the mud. It's like, 'Really?' And that was devastating. You grieve with your friends and your family and your colleagues when stuff like that happens because it's like, 'Wow,' because my heart just hurt for them.

George: How often do you think of Drew?

Steve: Every single day. Actually, I have two pictures of him I have a portrait shot that I took of him one day when he was unusually dressed; he had a shirt and a tie, and a jacket. I took a picture of him and his freshly braided hair and whatnot, so that's the screensaver. Then when you unlock the phone, there's a picture of him when we lived in Clinton, Maryland, which would've been prior to coming to Baltimore in '96, of him just clowning as a child. He has a plaid jacket and red and white stripe pants, like pants you'd wear on the 4th of July. One leg is blue stripe, one leg is red stripe. Those are the pictures that I have on my phone. Because the picture I did have was of my mother and her three grandchildren and me, but I changed that to this one.

George: Have you set up a shrine for him?

Steve: No, no. I mean the picture that ..., and [my wife], God bless her, was very helpful for me to get things together for his service. There's picture that's poster size upstairs in the living room, and in the dining room. Probably at some point, if I have an office where it'll fit, I'll probably put it there, but no shrine, I don't really function that way.

George: I confess, just outside of my office in the recreation room, I happened to have found pictures and I just started putting them on a desk I used to use, and Lord knows, it is filled with pictures. Not declaring it a shrine, but that's what it is. Anyway, how do you manage your grief?

Steve: I don't know. I did not shed a torrent of tears at the beginning. Every now and then, like today, I may have a few. I am comforted by the good news that we preach, that the grave is not the end of the story. At some point, I will get to see him again. There's no rush because I do have a nine-year-old.

I'm going to take my time with that. Yes, fourth grade, Sir. Nine-year-old.

George: There isn't a day that doesn't go by that I don't think of Chris.

Grief is like a wave that comes in sometimes unexpectedly. At one point it just overwhelmed me. I'm trying to be like a surfer so to speak, to ride it. I don't know when it's going to come, but when it comes, I try to ride the wave, rather than to get sucked under because I had a rough time of it. Being there when he passed, I felt a sense of powerlessness because there was nothing I could do for my child.

Steve: You're right. What was it that took him again?

George: It was renal failure.

Steve: Renal failure, right.

George: As long as I have my right mind, May 28, 2018, 04:15, Room 6, will always be etched in my memory. I guess that's what got me started on this path. It's something I can share with colleagues. I don't know of anything that has been written in the literature, but I guess in some small way, to help the younger colleagues who are coming in and those to come.

Steve: Yes, and then help colleagues that, unfortunately, may end up in this club nobody wants to be in.

George: I know you played a critical role in my time.

Steve: Yes, and again, everybody just ... and I don't know because I remember probably a few times during my ministry that I would talk about Job and when he went through all of that stuff. Then his friends came and saw him from a distance and then began to wail. Then after that, they came and sat with him, and then start saying stuff that people say, 'The Lord just needed another flower in his garden,' or I guess for Job, 'The Lord needed ten flowers in his garden, all of you children.' They just sat with him and didn't say anything. Then of course after that, [comes] the dialogue that gets more and more acerbic as you go.

Then eventually the Lord is like, 'All right, I've heard enough. You stand like a man and brace yourself. I got some questions for you.' His friends [i.e., Job's friends] just ..., this is a true ministerial presence because sometimes people are just like ..., 'I know you love me; I know you're concerned and you care, but just please stop talking.'

George: It's the attitude, yes.

Steve: Unfortunately, that did not happen with us. People just need us. 'We love you; we want you to know we're praying for you. Anything you need us to do, let us know. Take your time coming back, we got it.' That was about it.

George: Two questions, what triggers your grieving moments and who do you turn to?

Steve: It could be anything, nothing specific or in particular. It can be ... and this hasn't happened much because there's not that much interaction; I know [my former wife and her sister] both, they want to lay this at my feet. I've been very kind and restrained and will continue to do so, but please know and understand that I know that's absolute nonsense. You never know when a conversation there can go left, but again, that's just very, very, very, very rare, so it's really a non-factor. Nothing in particular. Every now and then, I will think about—Oh, music. Music, well, it doesn't trigger grieving, but it will be something that will make me smile.

Because I remember one of the times, a couple of times, I went over to Columbia to see him, and he really like music and so did I. He grew up listening to the music I listened to, and so we just sat in the car and just went through different songs in the playlist, and just talked about them and sat there and listened and enjoyed it. Some sense of regret because he was trying to put his life on a more ordered path, and he was actually supposed to be starting back at [a school of recording] and my mother was gifting him tuition to do that.

He was supposed to start in September or the beginning of October 2020, and so when I got the mail with the bill or the invoice for whatever the rest was going to be, and I called them [the school] just to say, 'so he passed away, he won't be coming.' Then, of course, they were shocked and very sorry for it. Then they did something I was not expecting. It wasn't a lot of money, it was maybe $150, whatever, but they sent the registration money back. [It was] Just some sense of regret there that he did not get a chance to live his best life. That he was trying to head in the right direction, make some changes, yes, do more structured preparation for the career that he said he wanted to pursue and one for which he had some gifts.

Just I get some regret attached to that, but it is what it is. Again, I'm just grateful that the grave does not have the final say because I always used to say whenever I die, either you get to heaven, so you got to check in with the Lord. You check in with the Lord and I said, 'Then after that,' the next words out of my mouth, 'Where's grandma?' I just said, 'Grandma's going to have to wait.' My first words will be, 'Where's my son?' and then, 'Where's grandma?' then everybody else. My son and I hope that he's the only one that I have to ask that question about children that were knitted together in their mother's womb because of me.

George: Do you find it difficult to do services for young people now?

Steve: I don't think I've had to do one. I've done more than I would like, but the Lord has used them every time for an outpouring of salvation. It's been phenomenal so much so that you will run out of the supplies that you have, the thing you want to put in a person's hands when they're there. There was a young lady who died. She was not a member of our church but connected to some of the folks there and she came by for some activities and ministry from time to time. She and her boyfriend were just playing around. She was supposed to be in school, but she was laying up with him, that's what teenagers do, it is what it is, but he had a gun. They were, I think, playing with the gun, and it went off and killed her. That service was at the church, and there was a packed house, a number of young people, high schoolers.

Then there was a young man who was nephew and cousin to a lot of my folks, a great kid. He, I think, was a freshman in college or a senior in high school, one of them. I think a freshman in college. Halloween, and he and three of his friends are going out to whatever, fun social event that eighteen, nineteen-year-old kids go to on Halloween. Coming in the other direction on a two-lane road where two adults who were drunk off their ass—[had a] head-on collision. His friends all lived, he did not.

They had the service at our church, and he was just beloved, just very well-liked by schoolmates, teachers. The sanctuary was packed. [There were cries of] People standing on the walls for two hours beyond the sanctuary into the narthex, a small area in the back of it, right out the back door of the church, and in the bigger narthex. People that came through just to greet the family, stretching under the parking lot, people for days, and to get the message. Check this, the parents of the people who killed him in the head-on collision were parents of a student at the high school he graduated from, and where his younger sister was a student, and I think in the same grade as their daughter.

People, well, misdirected their grief. I even said that I was like it was preventable, don't let any of us ever do likewise. That young lady has lost her parents, I think, both of them died. I think they're both dead. [She] Has lost her parents and she doesn't need to hear anything from anybody. It's like, what would the point be? I even told his sister, 'I can't tell you what to do, but I would like to suggest that if you are at the school and you see some people try to come for her, just go stand next to her and put your arms around her shoulder, and say, 'You know what? Ain't nobody got time for this. My brother's gone, her parents are gone, and y'all need to go somewhere and leave her alone.'

Just to say that those have proven to be very fruitful When Donnie passed away, I think over fifty people came. At this one other church that the young man passed, I was like, 'Okay, I need everybody to put down your email address, and we will send you something.' Because I have a letter that I have done for people who have given themselves to the Lord and to lift up some scriptures that they can check just as a foundation, as a launching pad for them. We sent out emails to as many people that gave us email addresses with the letter in it. I got an email back from one young lady, she said, 'I'm the young lady that was standing next to you when we were praying.'

We had a big circle. So, I just had everybody take hands and we were praying. I had a vague remembrance of a person who was shorter than me. A little White girl and I'm holding her hand. We're holding each other's hand and we're holding hands all the way around and she said, 'I was holding your hand when you were praying.'

I've had to do one for babies, who were less than two days old, in fact. One baby was probably less than two. One got killed by her mother's boyfriend, then the other just died for unknown reasons. He was in the care of a babysitter. No signs of abuse or anything, he just died.

I actually saw his parents at a surprise birthday/15th anniversary vow renewals for his older sister a few weeks back. He, and I don't know maybe because he is more grounded in the and in his faith, but he has, at least, the appearance of a more joyful—not at peace over this—but just having navigated as well as could be expected. She is having a much harder time with it. I saw them, I said, 'Let's sit down and talk, so I'm going to reach out to him so we can talk,' because it was making her, according to her sister-in-law, his sister lashed out and whatnot.

I know you're heartbroken, we get it, and you lash out at the people that are closest to you.

George: Yes.

Steve: I remember [a deceased colleague who dealt with terminal cancer]. He would lash out maybe a little bit at family, that's because family is closest.

[The conversation resumes regarding the infant child who died and the parents.] I don't know, just sit and talk to them. They have not been able to, as far as I know, conceive again.

I'm fine if I never ever, ever, ever have to do another service for a baby, a small child, a teenager, a young adult. That's not really the life we live or the world we live in.

George: I had both of those experiences. The first time was when serving my first church. I had never realized what it would be like to do a service for an infant. As soon as I took the family into the church for a private service, I still have etched in my memory of the little 'ornated shoebox [casket]' I called it, with this beautiful little doll inside. The next one was while I was at Smith Chapel, the same year Chris died. This sixteen-year-old, very vibrant, energetic teen who wanted to go into the JAG Corps, Air Force, and showing leadership roles in the junior ROTC, just dropped dead of a heart attack.

Steve: Wow.

George: That was in November 2018, and needless to say, when I went there, her lifeless body was on the gurney, and trying to be professional, I couldn't handle it. I had to call one of my Certified Lay Ministers [CLM] to come to be with me, and he carried on the service, but it just exacerbated my own grief. Have you shared your feeling with any of the other clergy members?

Steve: Yes, we talk. We'll talk sometimes. The thing is, and I'm sharing with you, that my two best friends [who died] were there [heaven] to greet my son when he got there, and I lost them like a month apart.

The people that you would talk to, and you could talk about anything, any way you needed to, you would never hear it again. In other words, it stayed between the two of you. That has, to a degree, been something that's missing, so you've just got to deal with it.

George: How's your family managing its grief?

Steve: I think as for his [Drew's] peers, it was hard—for my first cousin's children because they all grew up at the same time and would see each other at family gatherings and hang out from time to time—so it was hard for them. I did have an older first cousin who did because her son had cancer and died, and she actually died in 2019. She died less than a year before Drew did because he was at her service. Then the cousins that he was very close to on his mom's side, and of course, his sister and it's just … it's all ongoing. You have a moment where it'll grab you.

[Drew's sister] Lina's getting married January 1st and I'm imagining that there may be some, hopefully not many tears. That as well because that would be somewhere where he would've been and well dressed in his black tie and everything else. For Sophia [his nine-year-old from his present marriage], he [Drew] was the one that she had the better relationship with between the two; because he was always kind to her, but she did not know him well. I don't know, maybe just having a father who's a pastor, and so they can look at you sometimes just the way you dress going out of the house, 'Funeral?' [he laughs] 'Yes, it's a funeral.'

George: Are any of them in counseling? [Steve shares information not specifically related to the question.]

Steve: I have a colleague who knew him pretty well for much of his life that said that she had, I think, heard from him in a dream. She is one of those mystics among us who operates at that level. Ordinarily, I don't even remember, meaning, in general, let alone anything of mystical like that. She said that he came to her in a dream and just said, 'Tell my dad I'm okay.'

George: That's, I guess, one of my moments, I heard Chris' voice and he said, 'I'm okay, Dad.' I don't know whether there's something I'm suggesting to my conscience or am I really hearing or feeling from the afterlife?

Steve: You're not the only one who says that. When my best friend's brother died, because [it was during that time when] we actually started getting close, I was at the funeral. I didn't have a role, I was just there, a friend being supportive, and he said out loud, 'I don't have a brother anymore,' and apparently, I said, 'Then, well, I'll be your brother.' And that is in fact what happened. We became brothers, beloved to each other. Anyway, he said that he felt a squeeze, like somebody hugging him because his brother was bigger than he was. My mother talks about having felt a hand on her shoulder after my father passed away. [silence]

One thing that I would add is that for people who are grieving—who are maybe in a family situation that is no longer nuclear or ideal [familiar to them]—[those surviving family members] need to be gracious and kind and gentle with each other and allow each other the respect they need to grieve; and not use that as an opportunity to score points because there are no points to be scored.

We just need to try and be kind because, at that point, everyone is living their worst nightmare, and if that doesn't happen, then it diminishes, truncates, whatever other words you might want to use. [It] Exacerbates the grieving process for the person who was the recipient of the invective from the other grieving family member or family members. Of course, we know from our careers as pastors, families show their behinds at two times in particular and one of those two times ..., Reverend?

George: At the funeral.

Steve: Funerals, and what's the other time surprisingly?

George: At the wedding.

Steve: There you go. [he laughs] Funeral and weddings. Like wow.

George: Because Chris' mother and I, we were married for five years and after the third year, after his birth and what have you, we separated, and of course, waiting for the divorce papers to go through and all that. To be honest, I hated on Chris' mother, but at his death, it was the first time I had hugged her, and we hugged one another during that time, since the 1970s.

Steve: What year did he pass?

George: He passed in 2018.

Steve: '18, okay. That hug was a long time coming. [he laughs] Wow.

George: It was more of a time of sorrow.

Steve: Commiserating.

George: I was sobbing on her shoulder, and she was holding me. So, I guess, during that time, she was the stronger one between the two of us. In terms of her, I would say, she had coolness, being unruffled. See, that was the only time that I can remember on any occasion, well, maybe another occasion, it was just a formality when her mother passed and during the visitation at the funeral home, I gave her a perfunctory hug. That was the only other time. I think you're right in saying needing to be gentle with one another.

Steve: Yes.

George: Did you have to do any removal of his personal belongings from where he lived?

Steve: Yes, so that was another service, if you will, that I tried to render to his mom. The condo apartment that he was living in was one that she owned. I went into the apartment and cleared everything out. I got 1-800-GOT-JUNK to come. They took some things like the bedroom furniture that was in good shape, and then they would give it to a shelter or something like that. The other stuff that was trashed, they would just put out.

I emptied out his apartment so that his mother could get to what she needed to get to [for the purpose of selling it]. I just happened to be by there, some months later, just to see if it had been occupied by somebody else. There were people there doing renovation work. I had busted my hump to get it cleared out by the end of September 2020, and here it was 2021 and she hadn't done anything yet. But that wasn't my issue, it was her place.

[Referencing his son's belongings that he had cleared out, Steve says] I went through his stuff, the things that could go somewhere else, like a suit and some of his clothes, I took to the shelter over at First Baptist of Glenarden. They got a shelter the size of a warehouse in their outreach center. Then I went on about my life. In other words, that was all I needed to do.

[Sometime later, upon renovating his mother's house, Steve came upon special VHS tapes, one in particular, had Drew's voice on it, and showcased his musical talents.]

Steve: So, I found a cassette there that I made for my mom, which was one year when I went to the Hampton Ministers' Conference. It was funny because it was Drew's senior year, June of 2004, and his younger sister [Lina] says, 'Dad, you need to take him with you.' [he laughs at the remembrance of it all] she said that because it was Senior Week. That's when all the seniors go over to Ocean City and get torn up.

George: Oh yes.

Steve: She said, 'You need to take him with you.' And so, I did.

[Steve described all that went on during the Hampton Ministers' Conference, highlighting the Wailer Recital, a time when] People will sing or dance or do spoken word, or some kind of recitation, whatever, or play an instrument. Drew played and as a result of that, because he was going to be a freshman at Morehouse, there was somebody there who worked with the orchestra at Morehouse, and after they heard him play, they asked him some questions, he's like, 'Who are you studying with? Where are you playing,' or whatever and he didn't have an answer.

They said, 'Okay, why not?' Because of the skill they heard.

I have a photo, a video of him playing; so, he speaks, introduces himself and then he plays. I had that made into a DVD and I put one in the mail to [Drew's mother] and one in the mail to [his sister, Lina]. I have not heard from either, but that's fine. I didn't—I did not send it to them to get some attaboys or whatever. A thank you would've been okay, but life goes on.

Then I have some other ones here that I'm going to look through and there'll probably be some from [his] childhood through probably high school and I will have them put on DVDs as well and give them to them. I can look at those whenever I want and listen to his giftedness, playing the piano. [Drew] ended up getting a modest scholarship [about $4,000 or $4,500] toward his tuition at Morehouse.

I kept a sort of windbreaker jacket that was his, it fits me. [But] I gave most everything else away—shirts, slacks, a sport coat and whatnot that were [in good] enough shape.

My theological understanding about God has not changed. God has been gracious. God is faithful, and God's people evidenced their connection to God and then their life journey and some of them, of course, had lost children. That bringing to life, 2 Corinthians 1:3—5, where it says, [paraphrased] the comfort—that we will give comfort to others with the comfort we ourselves have received from God.

George: Yes.

Steve: And that's what happens.

That's in 2 Corinthians 1:3—5, and that's just, it's true that we pay it forward. You can never pay it back, but you can pay it forward because I told you, the woman who came over had a—had her car full of stuffed crab balls, a fruit tray, all kinds of things. Her daughter had passed away some years prior and I did her daughter's funeral and she's also lost a grandchild. Her granddaughter died at age two or three back in the '90s, I think before I got to Broadneck, but she still grieves her, because she will mention her sometimes on the prayer calls and I just wonder, she'd be twenty-eight now, I just wonder what she'd be doing, how she'd look, but you never know those things. She just came back in She didn't have much to say, she came and brought the stuff, hugged my neck, and left. Yes, but she ... so paying it forward, paying the kindness forward.

And I remember what Bruce said when JoJo died, he said another one of his friends who was a ministerial colleague, he said, 'You know that stuff you've been saying to everybody else for the last thirty years?' Bruce said, 'Yes'. He said, 'Do that.'

We're grateful for the company of people who love the Lord and our believers, and they can have the right word to say at the right time or no word at all. Just a hug in that—whatever is required.

George: Yes. I think about my niece, Tamara.

Steve succeeded me at my pastorate at Mt. Zion UMC in Baltimore from July 1996 to his current appointment at Asbury Broadneck UMC in 2006. And so, he was very familiar with my niece and all the congregants there. This next entry of his, he speaks of several young people who passed away at the church.

Steve: Yes, man, that still hurts. Of the three who died like back, to back, to back, that hurts the most because, unlike the other two who were sick and wore out, Donny had a donated liver and just was too sick to get another one. Then Randy had diabetes, it was out of control. Now he was not doing what he needed to do to stay here. For him to go that quickly with Tamara was just okay, you just made, you made a kid mistake, but it cost you your life.

So, when Tamara died, I just went to visit Dianna [Rev. DeFord's sister] at her house.

[Steve gives a recapitulation of the circumstances surrounding my niece's fatal accident.]

There are so many people that we've been pastor to, and God knows you don't want to come this way again.

George: Yes, sir.

Steve: You don't want to look at it all. You don't even want to be in a hospital thinking, 'Oh my God, it could happen,' you don't want to be anywhere near it. You don't expect to be exempt from life because you're living, you're here, this happens, babies die and everybody.

[What] pains you most when reflecting on the death of your child, I would just say, [a matter of] unfilled potential and regret. But I know that all things are made whole and made new where we're going. So, I hold onto that. Does he [Drew] come up as part of conversation? All the time and not in a grief-blatant way, but yes.

George: What is your statement of faith now in light of the death of your child?

Steve: God is faithful.

Well, I'll say this, I remember early when I started preaching again after he [Drew] passed. I said, 'I don't know how someone who is not in a relationship with the Lord could deal with something like this without losing their mind. I just don't know how they would do that.'

I am grateful for the relationship because as the disciples said when Jesus gave them the hard teaching and people started rolling out and he turned to them, 'Are y'all not going to stay, you're leaving too?' They're like, 'Where else would we go? You got the words of truth so where else would we go?' Where else would I go? There's nowhere else to go, God is faithful and has proven Himself, faithful, and God's people have been used by God to be a blessing in this time and seek Him.

George: Any further comments?

Steve: I don't think so. I think, no, I don't think so.

George: Well, thank you for your sharing on this. Indeed, I know some of the stuff that you have experienced, and it hasn't left, and I know it will come again.

Steve: Yes, it will.

Observations

Steve is a full member of the BWC with thirty-one years and is in his second marriage.

The sudden death of a thirty-four-year-old son of divorced parents has its own unique set of issues. The father of the deceased adult child is remarried and serves as a senior pastor of a suburban church in a community experiencing gentrification in a once predominantly historic

African American community morphing into a White upper income neighborhood.

Divorce inherently has its own issues of grief. With the death of the estranged couple's adult child, feelings of anger exacerbate toward one another. Notifying the mother of the child was problematic because the father initially contacted the sister of his estranged wife for the purpose of having someone with her when receiving the unthinkable news. However, the former wife felt that she should have been notified immediately. Anger occurs while the senior pastor/ estranged husband perceives that the deceased adult son's mother blames the father for neglecting his responsibility to tell her first, in person.

The celebration of the son's life occurs in two separate services. The pastor, upon encouragement from his bishop, attended the first service subsequent to seeing his son's remains before cremation; the second service took place at West River Camp Center, a favorite place of his son's.

Caring for the son's personal effects and property, the parents agreed to repair the town house and the removal of clothing and other personal items.

As of this writing, Rev. Tillet continues in grief counseling with a licensed clergy pastoral counselor. The Senior Pastor is a strong advocate for colleagues needing such help to navigate through the dilemma of personal grief.

Reverend Dr. Kay Albury

The Rev. Dr. Kay Albury, retired elder with forty-one years of ordained ministry, is a mother who has lost two sons. She set precedence as the first assigned clergywoman to serve long tenures in several United Methodist congregations. She served Ames United Methodist Church in Baltimore City in the area known as Sandtown, from 1985 to 2004, a period of nineteen years. During her pastorate of Ames UMC, Rev. Albury suffered the loss of her teenage son, Anthony.

Dr. Albury's next significant appointment, where she suffered the loss of her second son, was Saint Matthews United Methodist Church, Dundalk, Maryland. The said congregation of Saint Matthews is in a suburban milieu located in Turner Station, Dundalk, Maryland. Turner Station is an historic African American community in eastern Baltimore County.

Significantly, Saint Matthews UMC, founded in 1900, was the first church in the historically African American Community of Turner Station. The church's historical document reveals that the first cornerstone laid on May 10, 1910, but subsequently, the church moved to its present location on Avon Beach Road in Turner Station during the pastorate of the Reverend J.J. Thomas in 1927.

The Saint Matthews congregation has the reputation of being community-minded from its inception. The church was instrumental in getting streetlights for the community, a public school for its African American children, and it was active in the civic affairs of Turner Station. Also, ministries for youth and young people were central to the evangelistic mission for the members in addition to Christian development and foundation.

Dr. Albury averred that the church continued to play a vital role in the historical community of Turner Station, despite the onset of the COVID-19 Global Pandemic that affected many churches during 2020-2022. Presently, the average worship attendance (AWA) has been eighty-five congregants. The church is still working on maintaining a healthy and safe worship environment.

RESPONSES TO SELECTED QUESTIONS

Reverend Doctor Albury preferred to respond in writing rather than participate in a recorded interview. Pertinent to the death of her children, the pastor indicated one of her children suffered a prolonged illness while the other did not. Anthony, her first born died on September 28, 1985, after a two-year battle with a soft tissue cancer called synovial sarcoma. He was fourteen and buried in October 1985. Her other son, Lonzel, died at age forty-six of pancreatic cancer on April 29, 2019. His death came after a four-month battle. Lonzel had requested to be cremated.

"Cremation in the African American community is increasing vis-à-vis traditional burial practices," as cited in my second book, titled *Celebration, Life within the African-American Tradition* (2019).

Furthermore, the book goes on to inform, "The precedence of cremation was the subject of a 2016 news article in Charles County, Maryland, 'Based on a vital statistics report from the Department of Health and Mental Hygiene, there were 45,688 deaths among Maryland residents in 2014. Most were buried in a traditional casket. Still, more than one third opted for cremation...according to the Maryland Board of Morticians and Funeral Directors.' Executive Director Ruth Ann Arty reports, 'Hence, there is an increase of the use of cremation.'"

Eva Shaw, Ph.D. in her *What To Do When a Loved One Dies* is corroborated by the foregoing: "cremation in the United States is gaining wider acceptance, and the service is the choice for about 30 percent of all dispositions."

The cremation of Dr. Albury's adult son was not problematic for her, biblically and/or theologically as the practice is [becoming] normative for mainline denominations such as the United Methodist Church.

Reflecting back to the death of Anthony, Rev. Albury's first born, the immediate impact of his death drove her to seek help from the late Rev. Calvin P. Crosson, the long-serving pastor of John Wesley UMC, in Baltimore City. Rev. Crosson and his wife provided a private space for Kay to cry and express the anguish and pain caused by her son's death.

Dennis Apple, author, *Life After the Death of My Son*, comments about preconceived notions that ministers are not to grieve as typical congregants. He says, "Perhaps they had bought into the idea that believers, and especially ministers, have the hope of heaven and seeing one's loved one again. Therefore, we had no need to grieve our loss. (1 Thessalonians 4:13) Quite often, we hear Christians use this scripture to infer that because we have the confidence and hope of heaven, we should not grieve like the rest of the world."

Apple continued, "Christians are not emotional robots. If Jesus cried over the death of His friend Lazarus, we certainly have the right to cry over the death of our loved ones, too."

For Rev. Albury to go to the parsonage of the late Rev. Calvin P. Crosson, doing so offered refuge and catharsis during the initial stage of her grieving the loss of her son.

Both Ames and Saint Matthews UMCs and judicatory staff responded with compassion and support to Reverend Albury during the difficult times of her grieving and mourning. In her written response, she stated, "In both situations, the local church and conference administrative staff were very supportive. In 1985, Bishop Susan Morrison was my D.S. [District Superintendent] and strongly encouraged me to get counseling, as well as provided some financial assistance so that my family and I could go to Disney World, Orlando, Florida. Ames UMC in Baltimore was the church where I had just been assigned, earlier in July. They helped with tidying up the parsonage where we lived and providing meals daily for at least a week."

Dr. Albury following the death of her teenage son in 1985, did not take the necessary time off to grieve her loss

90

because in her opinion, working helped her get through the grief. It is not uncommon for some grievers to suppress their feelings through work.

Dennis Apple offers some enlightenment, as he stated, "As I look back, I realize I was starting to replace my deepest pain with busyness of my daily work schedule."

Kay confessed, "... and at thirty-five years old, I didn't know any better. [In] 2019, I did take some time off, not only from the church but completing my D. Min. I would say, I took at least a month," comments the pastor.

The matter of clergy entering into grief counseling relationship with a professional therapist is not widely accepted by some clergy. Nevertheless, Rev. Dr. Albury upon advice from her then District Superintendent, presently Bishop, Susan Morrison, took the advice which was ultimately beneficial. Further, her immediate family engaged in a three-month counseling session. For Kay, the counseling experience to use her words, "...was very helpful." However, at the time, she was uncertain that her late husband and remaining children benefitted from the process.

Dr. Albury intimated because of the death of Anthony, her teenage son, she, and her husband eventually divorced. Her situation was not unusual.

Author Janice Bell-Meisenhelder in her book, *Surviving the Unthinkable,* offers some insight, *"The catastrophic loss of a child imposes enormous stress on a marriage. Your* bond with your spouse will either grow incredibly stronger or be dissolved, depending on how you handle your grief and treat each other...Some people react by suppressing the pain as much as possible and by 'moving on,' which can be infuriating to the other parent, who copes with the same loss through uncontrollable crying [also]...couples who avoid talking to each other about their loss experience more grief..."

OBSERVATIONS

The Rev. Dr. Kay Albury, a retired clergy woman occupies a unique role in the Baltimore-Washington Conference of The United Methodist Church. She was admitted into the Conference as a deacon during the June 1979 session, becoming one of three ordained African American women pastors. She, indeed, was among the trailblazers. In June 1981, Rev. Albury was ordained as Elder and received into full membership of the annual conference.

Dr. Albury, whom I have known over the years, initially preferred not to participate in a recorded interview, opting to provide written responses to this writer's questionnaire. She was in the throes of completing her Doctor of Ministry project and did not want too much distraction. My next opportunity to confer with Rev. Albury was during her vacation and downtime from completion of the dissertation project.

Dr. Albury was open and spoke rather matter-of-factly about the losses of her sons. Although, she was more detailed about young Anthony's death in 1985. It was the late Rev. Calvin P. Crosson, pastor of John Wesley UMC, Baltimore City, and his wife, who offered Kay sanctuary in their parsonage home where she would grieve, or to use her words, "let it out," in privacy.

With the death of Lonzel, the pastor's adult son, who was forty-six, during the spring of 2019, Rev. Albury was less emotional, while also not having reservations about her son's final directive to be cremated.

My colleague, Rev. Dr. Kay Albury, is a seasoned pastor whose faith helped to navigate her through pastoral ministry, typically dominated by men. Anecdotally, I recall the occasion when she came to a pastors' meeting at a certain church, one of the pastors made the snide remark, "Is she the administrative secretary that will take the minutes?" Then the minister gave a mindless chortle. Ironically, Dr. Albury was pregnant at the time, and she was the only woman in that meeting. She has endured a lot.

Without hesitation, Rev. Dr. Kay Albury recommends grief counseling as one who had received the benefits of such counseling and suggests the service for those pastors needing the same help to confront their personal grief.

CHAPTER FOUR

A tale of two rural pastors:

THEIR EXPERIENCES WITH LOSS

OF ADULT CHILDREN

The accounts of two rural pastors who lost their adult children reveal the manner in which each dealt with the problem of facing personal grief, while serving local churches in rural settings of Southern Maryland. Both are in their senior years while one pastor is a widow and the other is in a blended family setting. Each pastor gives a glimpse of their way of managing the grief due to the loss of their teenage and adult children.

Pastor Eloise Newman

Pastor Eloise Newman serves Wards Memorial United Methodist Church, an African American congregation in the rural community of Owings, Maryland; she is a mother who suffered the loss of two adult children, sons, due to health problems. Pastor Newman began her ministry in 2009 at Wards Memorial and is a retired pastor with seventeen years of active service. She continues to serve the said rural congregation with an average worship attendance of 37 attendees.

Owings, Maryland is a Census Designated Place (CDP) in rural northern Calvert County, Maryland, with a population in 2020 of 2,483.

MY INTERVIEW WITH PASTOR ELOISE NEWMAN

George: This is Reverend George DeFord interviewing Pastor Eloise Newman. We will be interviewing Pastor Newman with her permission to use the materials that we gather during this time. Pastor Newman, you agree, is that correct?

Eloise: Yes.

George: All right. Let us begin. Pastor Newman, would you share your name, and we will move right into part one of the questions?

Eloise: I am Pastor Eloise Newman and I agree to this interview.

George: Thank you. For part one, it's my understanding that you've had two children who have passed. Is that correct?

Eloise: Yes, that's correct.

George: Beginning with the first child who died, what was your knee-jerk reaction to the news of your child's death?

Eloise: Shocked. It was sudden. I didn't see it coming. I think it was the first time that we had lost someone close, really close to our family. I think the whole family was in shock. As a matter of fact, I was on my way to Bible study, and I saw these two guys. I was getting out of the car with my daughter. They were friends of his ... and the look on their faces was—I can't even describe it. I'm saying to myself, 'I know these guys [are] not coming to rob me or anything.' They said to me, 'You need to come because Van [Vanderlee] is—,' I don't know whether they said sick or what, I can't remember. But I put my daughter back in the car seat and got back in the car.

I went to his apartment [where] he lived, I don't know whether you're familiar with it, across Suitland Parkway, in that area. [I was driving] The light caught me, and I really just wanted to ride out into the traffic because from where I was sitting at the light, I could see the ambulance. I thought maybe he was just sick. I don't really know what I thought.

When I got there, people were standing outside. When I came up the stairs, he was on the second floor, there were two police persons. One of them said to me, 'Your son had died or is dead.' I'm not sure what they said. I honestly can't remember what they said. I think, I don't know. I was out of it after that, and then when I got myself together, I went in. There he was, lying on the floor between the bedroom and the bathroom. It was just shock, I really could not ... It took me a while to even believe it was happening even after seeing him there.

After, I finally got myself together, I called my other children, I let my pastor know and people came. Everybody came because I think we all were in a state of shock. That lasts for a while. My whole family, we would just have to let go into the motion.

George: How old was your son at the time?

Eloise: My son was thirty. He had juvenile diabetes. I had read that at that time, children with juvenile diabetes, when he first got it, did not live past thirty. I kept that in the back of my mind, [because] it wasn't going to happen to us. But he was thirty.

George: Now, your next son who passed, what were the circumstances with him?

Eloise: He had cancer. He had prostate cancer, but by the time they diagnosed him, he was in stage four.

I saw him go from being such a nice-looking boy who cared so much about his appearance to looking like an old man. At that time, I think when he passed, he was fifty-nine, and that's been two years ago. He died in 2019. He was diagnosed in 2017, I think. By 2019, in the springtime, he was gone. I saw it coming. I saw this one coming, but even though I saw it coming, we were praying for his healing.

It wasn't the shock that I experienced with my oldest son. Matter of fact, they're my two older sons. The first one who passed was the oldest [Vanderlee]. The next one [James] was the number two sibling.

George: You were pastoring at the time when the younger son passed?

Eloise: Yes. Yes. Not the first one, but the younger one, yes.

George: In terms of the Celebration of Life, were your sons buried or cremated?

Eloise: They were both buried.

George: Can you recall the reactions of the congregation at that time?

Eloise: My oldest son [Vanderlee], when he died, I was still at Shaw [as a member of the congregation]. The people at Shaw rallied around our family. They were there night and day but being pastor at Wards was different. It was not that same kind of faith. I remember the Bible study did come on Friday and sat with me and they bought food and stuff, but that was it. That was it.

The thing that I remember most of all from both of them is that people will walk with you through, up to the funeral, get you to the funeral, and then they're gone. It is like, 'Now, you're okay because you buried them.' They were all there on day, night and day with my oldest son, night and day, all day, and I didn't have to do anything. Even when we went to the viewing, they were there, but the day after the funeral, everybody went back to business as usual.

With my son [James], since I was at Wards when he passed, there was none of that. There was nothing. The whole thing was just like, 'Oh, we'll pray for you.' I don't even know whether anybody said that it was just, 'I guess, you can handle it.' I don't know. I don't know the reaction.

The two reactions of the churches were so different in terms of being pastor. The reaction when I wasn't pastor was a whole lot different than the reaction being pastor.

George: What would you have wanted from the present church during your time of grieving?

Eloise: I think it's like just having somebody ask you, 'Are you okay?' and not to assume you are okay. Because you're not crumbling, you're not falling apart, nobody asks, 'Are you okay? How are you doing?' That would've been helpful. I think I've come to the conclusion that we often ask people how they're doing, but I don't think we really want to know because often I don't know that if I tell you, 'I'm falling apart.' Then maybe you don't know how to handle that because I'm supposed to be the one leading you. [They could be thinking,] *If you are going to fall apart, then I don't know how to react to that.* I don't really know.

George: What about colleagues during this last experience?

Eloise: [The bishop's assistant] came from the bishop's office. He called and he came. Other than Pastor Roosevelt [a colleague and friend at Shaw]—we grew up together—and there was another minister. That was it.

George: Did you take time off to mourn the loss of your children? I realize you have a congregation to care for.

Eloise: [She responded, yes and no.] Yes, but the first time I didn't. My oldest son died on a Friday, Sunday morning I was in church, and that was it. I can't remember what day my younger son died. I don't know what day that was, but no, I didn't take time off. The thing about it is it never even occurred to me to do it.

George: Have you sought counseling?

Eloise: No, I never felt the need to, not that I wouldn't, I just didn't feel the need to. I think if I was to experience that again, maybe I would, but at that time I just didn't. I don't have a problem with it. I just didn't do it, and nobody suggested that I do it.

George: By not taking advantage of grief counseling, it could negate even the opportunity to be in connection with others who are suffering the same situation. Do you agree with that?

Eloise: Right. I don't think I even thought about it. It just never occurred to me to do it.

George: In your opinion, and I hear what you're saying, but if you formulated an opinion, would you recommend group counseling or grief counseling for pastors?

Eloise: I think so because then it would give you an opportunity [to uncover] how you're really doing without anybody expecting you to be anything else—that it's okay if you fall apart. It's okay if you cry. It's okay if you take time. It's okay if you talk about what's going on with you. I think it would.

George: In terms of the length of time your first son passed and your second son, I guess that's in terms of years, how long was that? How many years?

Eloise: Oh, gosh. My oldest son died in 1985 and that's been quite a while. My youngest son, he died in 2019, so I still have my moments about that one, and sometimes they both crowd in [together].

George: I experienced the same thing. My son passed May 28th at 4:15 a.m. in 2018, and I've had my moments. At first, they were quite intense, now as time goes on it's not as often, but it comes, hence the reason I'm trying to work on this project because I'm wondering how many of us have deceased loved ones, particularly children. We are the caregivers and burden-bearers but when we have issues who bears our burden.

Eloise: Right. I just don't think people know how to handle you needing them.

George: I used the expression, 'That has passed as we keep our feelings covered inside of our robes.' You may have seen that. I suspect that we may feel within ourselves if we become emotive in the experiencing the anguish of our loved one's death, does that become an indictment against our faith? I have to remind myself, the scripture says, 'Jesus wept.' If our Lord can grieve, then what about us? Are there any moments that trigger your grief, or grieving?

Eloise: Sometimes it's a song, and it's not a song that has anything to do with him. [It's just a song or a moment or a TV show I'm watching, and someone else is experiencing and *it* brings tears. It just could be anything. It's nothing in particular.

It's not necessarily the birthdate because when my son's birthday came and my sister called me one Sunday morning, I was preparing to come to church. I was looking over my sermon as a matter of fact. She called me and she says, 'Well, we are remembering, and we just wanted to let you know we are remembering.' I was going like, *but I really didn't need that right then, right there*; because I did remember the days before that date but then when she reminded me that it was the date, because his birthday was September 5th, and that was first Sunday of September.

She called and my thing was, I think I got annoyed, and it was like, *why would you call me on a Sunday morning and ask me that?* I don't even think she thought about it [how that statement could be damaging in the moment]. I don't think it even occurred to her. I would've thought about it, I'm sure, during the day because I'd thought about it because I normally always tell Mike [a surviving son], 'I have three children left,' and I always tell him. 'Your brother's birthday is coming. And we remember, but on that day, which was his birthday, it wasn't in my mind until she called. It kind of messed me up for a while. I had to get myself together.

George: Have you conducted any funeral services for young people at Wards?

Eloise: No, I haven't. I haven't had any young people die. Not all were old but no young people.

George: How do you think you would handle such a situation?

Eloise: I don't know. I want to say, I don't think I would have a problem with it but I honestly don't know since I haven't had to do it. I want to say, I think I would be okay, but I don't know. I really can't say. I would like to say I would be there to comfort but I don't know what feelings that would conjure up for me. I don't know.

George: If I may just inject here. I don't know if this is what an interviewer is supposed to say to an interviewee, [chuckles] but my son passed in May and in November, one of our young, very promising teens, worship leader, bright scholar in school, and member of the Air Force Junior ROTC, suddenly passed. The family called me, and I naturally rushed to the ER where she was on the gurney, and it just felt like a mountain come crashing down on me that I was supposed to be there comforting them and I wasn't able to do so.

Even when I tried to perform my pastoral duties, I just broke down like a baby and I had to call the [Certified Lay Minister] CLM who I relied on. He came in right away and he had to do what I normally do but I was unable to do that because it just exacerbated my own grief. That's anecdotal too. How is your family dealing with this?

Eloise: I think we're all okay. My family, we're all okay. We talk about him, matter of fact, both of them. We remember certain things if we are together and thinking of something. We remember certain things and talk about it. It's not like the day never comes up. Whatever the situation is, we just go with it in terms of remembering who they were to us. It is not a hush-hush thing. We are able to talk about it. We are able to remember.

George: I have another question, personal effects of your loved ones, how long did you hold on to those personal effects? Or are you still holding on to them? I'm talking about clothes or things of that nature.

Eloise: Right. I didn't want anything, my youngest son, he started collecting things that he thought his brother would like in his new place and they're still downstairs. He hasn't gone through them. We plan to but even with that, I still don't think right now I want anything. I have pictures and I think that's enough.

George: What pains you most when you reflect on the death of your children?

Eloise: I think with my oldest son is that he had no children. He [Vanderlee] hadn't gotten married, and he had no children. I think about it now, how nice it would be to have a grandchild from him. My son [James] who died in 2019, he has a son and a daughter, and they're both married, and both have children. I think that was the one thing, that he didn't have, children, something you could put your hand on and say, 'This is him,' but he didn't have any.

I stay in touch with my grandchildren and my great-grandchildren because now they're married, and they have their own children. I try to be there for them as much as possible because their father's death was hard on them. It's the whole thing of trying to make sure everybody else is okay.

George: Has your theological understanding about God changed since the death of your children?

Eloise: Not changed but increased to the point that I know for sure, after losing my first son, I felt that l could get through anything. It wasn't that I wanted anybody to come pray for me. I really didn't need anybody to come give me scriptures and tell me, 'It's going to be okay.' I just knew God was there. I felt comfort. It was that way with both of them.

As a matter of fact, God sometimes shows me things in dreams. When my oldest son died, I had a dream. I was at a funeral. No, it was a wedding. It was a line, and we were going in the church to this wedding.

[The dream occurred when Vanderlee was in his thirties], but [in the dream] I had him in my arms. He was a baby. The wedding felt like a funeral, but it was actually supposed to be a wedding. A few days later that night I was on my way to church. For some reason I decided to go a different way. I ended up going to the church on the street where I brought him home. When I turned on that street, the feeling of death stepped over me.

Now, I can't explain to you what death is, what it feels like, [but] when it happened, I just knew that's what it was. I said to myself, 'Somebody has died.' By the time I got to the church and the guys were there and everything, it was my son, and then I remember. I tell you what I do believe now is that, in our relationship with God, He prepares us for stuff even when we don't know it.

When you get yourself together and you come back and you begin to think of things that you didn't see, or you missed and you go like, 'Oh, that's what God was showing me. God is getting me to understand.' It leads me to believe that God knew, and God was preparing me even though I didn't know.

Now, with my son [James] who died in 2019, I had a dream one night of people singing. They were singing with so much [power]. They were singing, 'Some glad morning when this life is over, I'll fly away.' Few days after that, I had a dream, and I saw my son which couldn't get out of bed. He was standing there, and he was home. There was this man talking to him. Beside him, was the wheelchair. When he passed, I wasn't shocked, but it was not what I was praying for.

I believe that if we pay attention to our loved ones when—and I've had experiences with people at church—when they say, 'I'm tired. I don't want to do this anymore.' We need to listen. I think that would help us. It would help us if we start to pay attention. I've learned that. In my ministry, one lady was taking chemo and she called me one day and she says, 'I'm not doing it anymore.' I simply said to her, 'If that's what you want to do then it's okay.'

I think when you hear people talk, it makes a difference to pay attention because in that way God is speaking to us, preparing us, and sometimes you don't even know it until afterward. These things come back to your remembrance, and you say, 'God was getting me ready for something I didn't even know.' I have learned that God warns us, God comforts us, and He sees us through. Regardless of the pain, I can say I got through it. Today, my faith is still intact. I might even say I'm a bit stronger.

George: Thank you for sharing that. What about your spiritual disciplines, your practices, prayer, meditation, scripture-reading?

Eloise: I talk to God. My granddaughter when she was younger, she used to say, 'Grandma, who are you talking to?' I would say, 'I am talking to God.' As the years went on, she doesn't ask me anymore if she hears me talking and nobody is here but me. She knows, and she says, 'Are you talking to God?' and I say, 'Yes.' [Eloise's daughter is a pastor as well.]

I love God's Word. There's a scripture that is, praying and talking to God, it's that whole relationship with God. I can share now how I'm feeling on a certain day and that helps. The Word helps, the singing of songs help, the reading the Word and just reading inspirational things, all of those things help. Sometimes people help you when you're not even thinking about it, you hear something, and you get hold of it. It's almost like [God saying], 'I want you to hear this.' It's just out of the blue somewhere.

George: Are there any other comments that you'd care to share?

Eloise: I don't know. One of the things I have learned, and it might seem a bit harsh with some people, but life goes on. You cry. There's that song I think CeCe Winans [a contemporary gospel singer] sings, I don't know who it is, but it's somebody. It says, 'Don't cry for me.' I don't like that song. I think you ought to cry if that's what you're feeling. I tell people, 'Feel what you're feeling.'

Cry if you have to, and cry till you can't cry anymore because every time you cry, you feel a little better.' I think that is God's gift to us, the ability to cry. What it does is relieve us. It gives us certain relief because after you finish crying you feel like, *I can go on a little more. I 'm okay for right now.*

We can't deny the feeling. It's there. I don't care whether you are in the pulpit preaching or what, the feeling is there. You can't deny it. To deny it, I think it might even make you sick, to try not to let that all come out. Just let it happen. I remember my first son when he died, I cried every morning. Every morning, I cried. I cried. Everybody in the house knows I cried.

Psalm 121:1-2, I think it is, says, 'I look to the hills from whence my help comes. My help comes from the Lord who made heaven and earth.' I was reading that scripture because I heard it during the funeral service. And I *heard* it. I was reading it every night. One night it was almost as if the words jumped off the page and it shocked me to my core. It says the God that created heaven and earth said He would help me.

The next morning, I didn't cry, and I got better after that. It was almost like, 'I'm going to help you, I will help you get through this no matter what it feels like, but I will help you.' I thought that was so profound, and I tell folks that even today God is true to His Word. If we let Him, He will help us through whatever it is we need to get through. Nobody said it's going to be easy. It's not always easy, it doesn't always feel good. But a good cry helps. It just helps it. I think that's God's gift to us—tears.

George: I say too, God has given tears to us. If He didn't mean for us to have tears, then He wouldn't have given them. It is all part of our formation. It's a catharsis to us, for us. Well, I thank you very much for sharing this with me. In a sense, we are on the same journey when it comes to the loss of a child or children. There's a certain commonality of experiences that you have experienced. And I have experienced.

I think as I was reflecting, colleagues don't share. Hence, I say that they keep it inside their robes and show this facade or veneer, whatever you want to call it, this mask of strength and absolute faith. But in particular, it was some of the male pastors. As I said, before, if Jesus wept, so can we. I hope that I would be able to bring this together in a form that will be helpful to others—clergy.

I don't know, you may have said this, but it just popped into my mind, as a pop-up. In your opinion, and it may be on the questionnaire that in terms of grief counseling, do you feel that clergy should be with clergy in terms of the group counseling experience or grief counseling?

Eloise: Not necessarily. I think if you need therapy and you need a good counselor, maybe. I don't necessarily think it has to be clergy, especially, if it's clergy who has not experienced the same thing. Your therapist might not either. I don't think it's necessary to have [separate] group counseling—if the people in the group [clergy and nonclergy] are experiencing the same thing. I think that would be great. But if it's just a bunch of people coming together, and not having had the same experience, I'm not sure.

George: A commonality of experience?

Eloise: Yes. That means you can help each other because *I know, I understand.* While I can't exactly say you feel what I feel, you feel grief and at the time, that's what I feel.

Do we have grief counseling in our [denominational] office?

George: Well, that's a question that I have also because I went to a grief counselor who was connected with a hospice program. I don't know. I suspect that the benefits office would give you the authorization to seek out your own counselor. That's my thinking right now. I don't know until I call to ask. That's what prompted the question of clergy coming together. That need for grief counseling for clergy only, would that be a suitable situation?

I guess you're talking about an affinity group where-I don't know. That's just a thought and I don't know how it would be received, but it remains to be seen. I think also that some clergy just do not reach out. My own personal experience, that even after the death of my son, I continued to work at the church. Looking back for me, I should have taken some time off. You were a social worker before going into ministry?

Eloise: Yes.

George: You may have learned from some of your classes about group counseling and some of the terms of transference and countertransference, that sort of thing. I just had a brief observation, I guess I really wasn't focusing on it. As the pastor grieves, so the church grieves, I think. You've brought up an interesting point about, what was the response to your circumstances. You were on target also when you said that, not your exact words, but its perfunctory people who'll ask how you're doing instead of those who will ask when they really don't want to get caught up in 'your circumstances' because of their own fears.

Eloise: They want you to be okay—yes.

George: The other thing is that people will bring to you, a lot of platitudes, saying, 'Well, God meant this to happen.' I had begun to think—and you will have to pray for me on this—, *I don't want to hear anyone saying that God knew the road was getting rough*, and so forth and so on. I think people will just offer that as trying to be consoling when really, they're not. It's a vacuum. It's empty.

Eloise: I don't think they know how. They don't know how.

George: No, they just say things.

Eloise: The one [comment I dislike] is 'God look down in the garden and wanted to pick the rose.' Oh, no, I hate that. I absolutely hate that. [she laughs]

George: About these empty platitudes, or even some overworked biblical platitudes, that folk sometimes spout out, I believe that no harm is intended. I think about Job when his friends came, they were doing well when they were sitting and being quiet. It was the moment that they opened their mouths; they messed up.

Eloise: That's it.

George: Sometimes you just need somebody just to sit there and listen.

Eloise: That's all.

George: I hope and pray these things you have shared during this interview will be of value to clergy. Thank you for your graciousness and sharing with me your experiences with loss. I know that every now and then those waves of grief will come. I think it's God's grace that helps us to serve through these experiences of life. The waves will continue to come, but He gives us the sustaining grace to deal with it.

Thank you and God's blessings.

OBSERVATIONS

With the loss of her first son, Eloise described her emotional response to his demise. She openly mourned his death without apology. In response to her mourning, the parishioners of A.P. Shaw UMC were compassionate as expressed through their various acts of kindness. However, in contrast, her current rural congregation, while well-meaning, did not come to the level of her home church, A.P. Shaw. The rural church made its customary expressions of condolences to the pastoral family void of the depth of compassion as shown by A.P. Shaw.

It is important to note here that there are several variables at play. When Eloise suffered the loss of her first child, while at A.P. Shaw, she was not clergy, but a layperson. When she suffered the loss of her second child, she was clergy. Could the different responses call out how members of a congregation perceive the needs of one who is among a congregation versus one who is clergy?

Eloise continues in pastoral ministry as a retired local pastor, meeting the needs of the rural congregation in Owings, MD. This senior retired clergy woman with a professional background in social work readily recommends grief counseling to members in bereavement, yet reluctantly seeks such services for herself. Paradoxically, as it seems, the pastor seeks help for her grief solely through prayer and reading the Holy Scriptures. Perhaps she relies upon this scripture, "But I would not have you to be ignorant, brethren, concerning them who are asleep, that ye sorrow not even as others who have no hope." (1Thessalonians. 4:13, KJV).

I speculate Eloise is a part of that generation of older pastors who steadfastly rely upon their faith in God and prayer to confront the inner emotional turmoil of grief caused by the death of their loved ones. Moreover, to exemplify her faith as a spiritual leader, she refrains from seeking counseling from a professional grief counselor or therapist. Pastor Newman is a classic example of older generation pastors.

PASTOR IRVIN E. BEVERLY

Pastor Irvin E. Beverly is the longest serving supply pastor since July 2000 of the historic Bethesda United Methodist Church, located in Valley Lee, Maryland, an unincorporated community in rural St. Mary's County, Maryland. The church organized one hundred and ninety-three years ago as a White congregation; built prior to the Civil War. It was destroyed by fire by an arsonist. According to the church's historical documents, the White parishioners did not rebuild the original edifice.

The trustees of Bethesda after the Civil War negotiated with Black members to build a church on the northwest corner of the vacant property. According to the church's general history, the African American congregation built its house of worship, circa 1866, although the land officially transferred, circa 1885, and enlarged, four years later, as a result of the gift of over an acre of land by George Scott. The present structure was constructed in 1911.

Over the years, physical improvements added to the building. In 1976, a vestibule [narthex] was constructed in memory of the Lawrence Family. The congregation erected a social hall and dedicated the same on October 26, 1991; the new space provided the members an opportunity to conduct various ministries outside of the main sanctuary and enhanced community ministries, i.e., Soup and Sandwich ministry for the homeless and social functions for neighbors in the surrounding community. Other improvements occurred as the pastor and trustees deemed necessary to meet the demands of ministry and to keep up with current technology.

SUMMARY OF PASTOR IRVIN E. BEVERLY'S RESPONSES

TO SELECTED QUESTIONS

Pastor Irvin E. Beverly is the personification of the quintessential African American rural pastor. He is well-known as a preacher who preaches with spiritual fervor; notably during his sermon delivery, he asks the rhetorical question: "Did I say that right?"

Pastor and Mrs. Eileen Beverly, married for twenty-nine years, suffered the loss of their sixty-year-old daughter, Bridgette, during the summer of 2022. Their daughter succumbed to a prolonged illness. "We were expecting it to be a short time in the future, but not that soon," answered Pastor Beverly. At the time of their daughter's death, the pastor was in his mid-eighties while his wife was in her mid-seventies.

Reflecting upon the reactions of the local church, the leadership of the Baltimore-Washington Conference, and clergy colleagues, Pastor Beverly expressed how he was, "surprised," to describe his overall feelings to the expressions of compassion and empathy for the family's grief.

Dr. J. Cogman, District Superintendent, clergy colleagues, in addition to flowers, gifts and visitation, all came as a compendium of care from the general church. The rural pastor recalled how he once expressed a different kind of sentiment. He conceded how he had once sarcastically opined, "...the conference doesn't care about us in small country churches." So, when Irvin and Eileen, comprising of clergy, spouse and parents, "experienced the outpouring of Christian love through the many expressions of comfort, love, and comradeship," the Beverly's were no longer among the disgruntled.

Pertinent to the pastor, spouse/parent's emotional feeling about the death of their daughter, ambivalence best describes their feelings. There was relief that their child's painful suffering was over, but they were, "...highly grieved..."

The lingering effects of grief due to the death of the Beverly's adult daughter, continues to be fresh. Irvin, despite the lingering feelings of sorrow, continued with his pastoral duties and responsibilities; he chose not to follow up with taking grief counseling or a period of rest from his duties as recommended by the denominational judicatory. However, he recommended bereaved families of his local congregation to take advantage of the professional services of a grief counselor. Possibly, Pastor Beverly ascribes to the notion that pastors should depend upon their spiritual strength and discipline of prayer in contrast to use grief counseling as a resource. Also, there is no hint of that Irvin will recommend to his colleagues with similar circumstances to join an affinity group of pastors wherein they could share their personal struggles with grief. Such a setting would be meaningful in terms of managing their grief.

The lingering effects of grief have no expiration date. Pastor Irvin responded to my inquiry after five weeks when he could finally get to the point of thinking of his deceased daughter, "very often, not daily."

However, for most, the lingering effects of grief can remain strong even though time has passed. For example, the senior pastor of Hope United Methodist Church, Southfield, Michigan, the Rev. Dr. Benjamin Kevin Smalls, commented, "All I did was take [his mother and grandmother's] pictures from the kitchen to my office. That's all I did. And tears came out of nowhere. Missing these two more than ever."

It had been twenty-one years since his mother's death and eight years since his grandmother's passing, still, Pastor Smalls intimated, "But when I have these moments, which apparently won't cease, I feel their embrace and love in large doses. I sense some of you know of this."

In moments when the sorrowful emotions manifest, the rural pastor, Pastor Beverly, said, "[I] always turn to the Bible and prayer."

Another practice mentioned by Pastor Beverly was the act of grieving together as his family reminisced about their beloved daughter.

Retrospectively, the clergy-parent points to certain moments and activities that trigger their painful memories. And because of Bridgette's recent demise, the grief continues to be very fresh in the family's mind. It is interesting that the immediate family members did participate in grief counseling although the pastor did not indicate where or with whom.

Pastor Beverly was reticent about sharing and dealing with his feelings of grief with clergy colleagues. Curiously, he suggested that he would recommend grief counseling to his colleagues. However, the notion of *Take your time of difficulty to God on your knees,* was the method he used. It is succinct advice present in the hymn, *Leave it There.* Its refrain espouses *Take your burden to the Lord and leave it there.*

Pastor Beverly's advice echoes writer Anne Cetas' meditative comment in *Our Daily Bread*, September 2022: "During our times of grief, God's love remains steady; We always have Him to lean on as we lean on and love others in His strength."

The sole solution with addressing the dilemma of personal grief in Irvin's view is absolute faith in God working out the problem. And for him and his wife, the memorabilia that once served as triggering mechanisms of grief and pain, now serve as loving memories and relief that their daughter no longer suffers from her illness.

Pastor Beverly's unadulterated faith is remarkable. The matter of theodicy could be raised: "Why does a good and righteous God permit tragedy to happen to God fearing servants?" The rural clergy-father is Jobian-like in his attitude: "...the Lord gave, and the Lord has taken away, blessed be the name of the Lord," (Job 1:21b).

EXCURSUS

The Celebration of Life service for the daughter of Pastor Irvin and Mrs. Eileen Beverly was consistent with the ethos of African American funerary practices. The service occasioned at the First Missionary Baptist Church, Lexington Park, Maryland where the Rev. Roderick W. McClanahan, is the senior pastor. The parking lot was at capacity, resulting in vehicles parked in any vacant spot on the campus of the church. Similarly, the sanctuary was at capacity notwithstanding keeping within the boundaries of the CDC parameters of social distancing, preventing the possible spread of COVID-19.

The worship service lasted more than two hours, while the participants faithfully followed the order of service. Visiting clergy and the district superintendent were recognized. The participating clergy did not stray off point by giving their own sermonettes.

Pastor Beverly eulogized his daughter with an arousing message, titled *Going to the Other Side,* based upon Matthew 14:22-27 with emphasis on, "go on ahead to the other side," (verse 22b). In his characteristic rhythmic, sermonic style, the pastor laced together the account of Jesus walking on the water toward the other side of Lake Galilee and his daughter transitioning into eternity. Periodically during his delivery, he paused and rhetorically asked, "Did I say that right?" (The distinctive style of his preaching.) To which, there was talk-back from the congregation, an expectation in the Black Church worship experience. To say the least, there was a spiritual fervor enveloping the worshipers as the preacher-father came to a rousing climax: "She's on the other side now!"

The funeral service for Bridgette was celebratory and not mournful in the traditional sense. There was no outward show of emotional distress rather more revival-like. At the conclusion of the service, the processional music was upbeat with the singing of, *When We All Get to Heaven* as the clergy, pallbearers under the guidance of the funeral director led the family out of the sanctuary. The waiting limousines attendants assisted the family into the cars that prepared to form up for the funeral cortege and journey to the cemetery, where there would be a committal service and finality to the mourning ritual.

OBSERVATIONS

Pastor Irvin E. Beverly, a well-known rural pastor of an historical African American United Methodist Church in St. Mary's County, MD, is the church's longest serving pastor. He and his wife, Eileen, have a blended family. His daughter, by marriage, transitioned during the summer of 2022 due to the result of a prolonged illness.

The pastor, in his mid-eighties, is the personification of the quintessential rural pastor who opted not to receive the services of grief counseling. Leaning on his unwavering faith, he solely depended on God to help him through the grief and mourning for his adult daughter. His choice of taking *his problems to the Lord* typifies the general attitude of pastors who do not want to trouble their colleagues or disclose their need for help during a painful time. This is the dilemma most pastors face when encountering personal grief. Also, in a denomination where a judicatory has the authority to assign a pastor to a congregation, a disclosure such as taking grief counseling could be construed as a negative, thus impacting upon a pastor's career path and effectiveness for ministry. Hence, most pastors will, *stuff it inside their robes* while maintaining a façade of strong faith and spirituality—hoping not to be stigmatized or seen as weak, or out of control of one's faculties.

My immediate impression of Pastor and Mrs. Beverly, as a senior couple grieving the loss of their adult child, is that they are of strong faith steeped in African American traditions when it comes to religious values._This couple presents an earnest and simple faith in Jesus Christ. In fact, I suggest, "[one could] recognize [he/Peter] had been with Jesus," (Acts 4:13). So, Pastor Beverly's faith *should* sustain him and his wife. Perhaps they both feel, during their moments of grief and mourning, that their belief would remain intact, dutifully referencing the psalter: "Cast thy burdens upon the Lord and He shall sustain thee; he shall never suffer the righteous to be moved," (Psalm 55:22 KJV); and 1Peter 5-7, "Cast all your anxiety upon Him because He cares for you."

Please note that my observations of their responses to my questionnaire also consider the grief and mourning of the decedent's immediate family consisting of her husband and children.

But I would love to dig a little deeper. Responding to my questionnaire, Pastor Beverly stated that while he rejected the idea of seeking counseling for himself, he had referred many of his congregants (in similar situations) toward counseling. Could this suggest that he was amenable to counseling and recognized the value of grief counseling?

I submit a recapitulation of his thoughts on the subject: The lingering effects of grief due to the death of the Beverly's adult daughter, continues to be fresh. Irvin, despite the lingering feelings of sorrow, continued with his pastoral duties and responsibilities; he chose not to follow-up with taking grief counseling and a period of rest from his duties as recommended by the denominational judicatory. However, he recommended bereaved families of his local congregation to take advantage of the professional services of a grief counselor.

***

This is a new exploration into the topics of how clergy decide to handle grief, therefore specific data is either difficult to find or simply nonexistent. That said, it is my belief that Rev. Beverly typifies those members of clergy who are not inclined to take grief counseling based upon their understanding of Holy Writ. The apostle Paul articulated, "But we do not want you to be uninformed ... about those who have died, so that as others do who have no hope ..., (1 Thessalonians 4:13 NRSVUE)." Contra to Pastor Beverly, younger pastors are open to receive the professional help of a grief counselor or therapist. Whereas younger pastors are open to receive the professional help of a grief therapist. It's a changing trend that, in my opinion, needs further study.

Chapter Five

A Look at Clergy Grief and The Extended Family

Thus far, I have discussed situations experienced by immediate family members of clergypersons. Now, I'm turning my attention to clergy who are members of a kinship group impacted by the loss of a grandchild and a nephew. The clergy in this said situation encompasses a category of ministers whose unique circumstances deserve attention. The grief of ministers who suffer the loss of their children is not limited to the immediate family—its nucleus. Such grief has the power to engulf extended family members, and friends and associates besides. As a result, I'm addressing the matter of a retired clergy grandmother who suffered the loss of her granddaughter, right alongside with her adult daughter and son-in-law. Next, I present the account of an active full member clergy who is an aunt serving in the Baltimore-Washington Conference of the United Methodist Church.

Rev. Dr. Sue Shorb-Sterling

The narratives reported thus far, pertain to young and adult children of clergy and their parents' painful responses to their death. However, little is said concerning clergy grandparents and the trauma experienced by them when losing a grandchild(ren).

I turned to the devastating loss of the granddaughter of the Rev. Dr. Sue Shorb-Sterling, Retired Member (RM) with twenty-two years of active service in the Baltimore-Washington Conference of the UMC. It demonstrates the swirling currents of grief that pulls other family members into its grasp.

Dr. Shorb-Sterling served Salem UMC, Brooksville, Maryland prior to her retirement. Salem UMC is a predominately White congregation. The church was established in 1833, when Brooksville was an isolated farming community in Montgomery County, Maryland. Now, the area is Olney/Brooksville, a suburban community. Yet, Salem UMC continues to maintain a family church culture with an average worship attendance of sixty-five as reported in 2015.

Sue initially agreed to interview with me but opted to complete the questionnaire because her daughter and son-in-law continues to grieve their loss, it's still too painful to talk about their ten-year-old daughter's death. Therefore, the responses to my two-part questionnaire (its subsections, titled *The Initial Grief and Mourning Responses, and the Lingering Effects*) are captured in verbatim.

Sue described her reaction to her granddaughter's death and how the family reacted. "Our granddaughter at the age of 10, went into septic shock three weeks prior to her death. During those three weeks, she was placed on ECMO because the inner lining of her lungs was damaged. ECMO stands for Extracorporeal Membrane Oxygenation which oxygenates the blood outside the body so the heart and lung can heal. She also had each leg removed a few days apart because of septicemia. I had hoped she would survive. We all wanted her to survive. We knew she would have a really difficult fight to regain her health. But deep down, I knew that it was just a matter of time. I just didn't know exactly when the phone call would come.

When I received the phone call, my first thought was of my daughter, son-in-law, and the surviving granddaughter. They had been through so much during those three weeks. And now, she was gone. I suppose you could say I was 'braced for the inevitable,' but it hit me hard. I also knew I needed to be strong for the rest of the family: my husband, my daughter, my sons, and the remaining grandchildren.

Since our granddaughter died on Good Friday, one of my first thoughts was the need to get pastoral coverage for Easter Sunday. I called my D.S. and asked him if he could find coverage for me, so I could focus on my family and my grief. About fifteen minutes after I called him, he called me back and said that he couldn't find anyone to cover Easter Sunday. So, while my son drove us to the hospital, I was on the phone to find an elder who could preach and officiate communion on Easter Sunday. And I did.

Our family gathered around and supported each other as best we could. Each person dealt with the news and the grief differently."

The retired pastor rendered more details that led to the death of their 10-year-old granddaughter. She shared, "Our granddaughter contracted a rare bacterial infection that quickly turned septic. She went into respiratory arrest several times. Each time she was resuscitated, however, because of the lack of blood flowing to her extremities, the tissue in her legs began to die. She died three weeks after the first respiratory arrest."

Both Sue and her husband were in their mid-to-late sixties while her daughter was in her early forties. Addressing the matter of burial or cremation, Sue simply wrote "Our granddaughter was cremated." She did not expound further on the practice of cremation.

The Salem UMC congregation was quite empathetic with the Shorb-Sterling family as reflected in Sue's comments, "The congregation whom I served at the time was a group who believed in the power of prayer. Part of our worship time was devoted to praying for the sick and hurting. As our family was walking through those three weeks, I gave updates each Sunday on my granddaughter. They knew her, too. When my daughter visited with us, she and her family attended worship. So, the congregation saw our granddaughter grow up from a small baby into a bright, talented 10-year-old girl. Not only did this congregation pray corporately, but also, individually for our granddaughter.

"When word was sent out on Good Friday that our granddaughter had died, I received so many texts and voicemails expressing their condolences and grief. My loss also became their loss. The elder who led the Easter worship that Sunday told me that some were angry that God did not answer their prayers for healing. He had to reassure them that God always hears our prayers but doesn't always answer them the way that we want. He also told me that many in the congregation were struggling to celebrate the Resurrection in the midst of grief and sorrow. He offered comfort that in the midst of our death, Christ's Resurrection promises us resurrection and eternal life.

"I did not attend worship with this congregation on Easter Sunday. I didn't want the attention to be on me. Instead, I went with my daughter-in-law to her church and cried through the entire worship. I was numb, just numb with disbelief and grief."

The days following the loss of Sue's granddaughter was a time of quietness, silence at meals and talk only when necessary. Numbness overshadowed the family. Sue wrote, "I already had planned to take the week after Easter off. So, I spent that week with my daughter, son-in-law, and surviving granddaughter. I tended to their needs as best as they would allow me. Mostly we sat around being quiet, staring into space, making a meal, and eating in silence, or reading. No one wanted to talk. The only time we really talked was when we were planning the memorial service for the following weekend.

"Since it was springtime and my daughter lives in the woods, I spent many quiet hours sitting on her porch swing looking out over the woods. I saw my granddaughter everywhere. She loved playing outside and she loved springtime. And I remembered the springs in which we hiked through the woods looking for specific plants coming to life."

As mentioned earlier, the judicatory leadership responded to Dr. Shorb-Sterling, its lack of success to find Easter Sunday coverage. To that, she commented, "I was so disappointed!" She had made the urgent request, she wrote, "Before we had our bags packed to travel to be with my daughter.

"In the years I had been a pastor, I don't think I ever asked my D.S. to be pastoral for me. I couldn't believe that he spent only a few moments calling available elders and didn't continue until he found someone. I needed him to act on my behalf at that moment! I think about this often. What would I have done if I would have been a D.S. receiving this news? I think I would have moved heaven on earth to find someone so that the pastor didn't have to take on this responsibility in the midst of dealing with the death of a family member. And if I couldn't find someone, I would have changed my plans and stepped in to be with this congregation during this time of grief.

A few days after Easter, I received a voicemail from the bishop offering her condolences and a prayer. I still have it saved on my voicemail. I think this was the only time in my twenty-three years as a pastor that I had a bishop call me."

The pastor received calls from colleagues and their empathetic reactions. Here Sue described well-meaning individuals who wanted to be supportive by expressing their concerns yet making blunders:

She shared, "I am *friends* with many colleagues on Facebook. Through this media, many offered their condolences. The passing of my granddaughter was posted on the weekly eConnection. A few sent me sympathy cards probably from reading about it there.

"The Annual Conference occurred at the end of May which was about six weeks after my granddaughter's death. I did not expect to have so many come up and ask me how I was doing. I emotionally couldn't handle it. It was the wrong question. How do you answer a question like that? *How do you think I am doing? I am numb. I hurt. I want to cry out, 'Why, God?' No, I am not doing fine.* If one more person asked me how I was doing, I was going to scream! I remember trying to avoid people I knew. I remember after one encounter turning around and going back to my room and staying there. I ate in my room so I wouldn't have to interact with people.

A good friend of mine lost her father that year. She is the wife of a colleague. She asked if we could sit together during the Memorial service, which we did. I was fine until the celebrant invited us to say out loud the names of those, we knew who died. I remember saying through tears to my friend, 'I can't say her name!' And she said, 'No worries, I will.' Somehow for me, saying her name made her death final. I know that sounds crazy. I knew she was dead. I touched her body and kissed her forehead. I was at her

Memorial service but saying it out loud at that moment made it way too real and final. I gave my friend a hug and left to go to my room before the Memorial service was over, so I didn't have to speak to anyone.

Her feelings are quite consistent with what Dennis Apple commented, "… Sometimes I wish people would just leave me alone." He explained, "… a person who's grieving the loss of someone in his or her life must be given space and time to grieve … dare they try to rush this process. It takes as long as it takes."

Also, Apple commented, "I listened to them, and secretly wished they would finish what they had to say and move on – out of my presence …."

Andy Randie of the Northumbria Community wrote in *Common Prayer: Liturgy for Ordinary Radicals*, "Do not hurry as you walk with grief; it does not help the journey. Walk slowly, pausing often; do not hurry as you walk with grief. Be not disturbed by memories that come unbidden. Swiftly forgive; and let Christ speak for your unspoken words. Unfinished conversation will be resolved in Him. Be not disturbed. Be gentle with the one who walks with grief. If it is you, be gentle with yourself. Swiftly forgive; walk slowly, pausing often. Take time, be gentle as you walk with grief."

Dr. Shorb-Sterling described her role with the preparation of the funeral service. Sue stated, "My daughter and son-in-law had a pastor and a church; however, the week I was with them, they would often consult with me about concerns and ask questions about the Memorial service. I was grateful I could be of some assistance, help them navigate what they wanted for a Memorial service and what would be meaningful to them. In many ways I felt helpless after our granddaughter's death but being able to tap into my pastoral experiences with funerals made me feel somewhat useful to my family.

Taking sufficient time off for mourning before returning to pastoral duties is a necessity. Pastor Shorb-Sterling addressed this matter as follows, "I had already planned to take a week's vacation after Easter. I had a lay speaker planning worship and preaching. I followed through with these plans but was back in the pulpit on the Second Sunday after Easter. No, I didn't take any time off to mourn. By the middle of the summer, I was done with preaching and being a pastor. All I wanted to do was spend time with my daughter and surviving granddaughter and my other children and grandchildren. As pastors who work weekends, it is difficult to find time to spend with family when they have off work on weekends. I had missed many family functions because of my weekend pastoral schedule. The family had sacrificed enough! I consulted with my children about the possibility of retirement. They were enthusiastic. So, I planned to retire the following July.

"I often wondered what I would have done if retirement hadn't been looming so close on the horizon. Would I have been able to ask for some time off? Would the church (and Conference) have given me the time needed? I know of no jobs where one can take extended time to grieve and mourn. Often the employee is given just the day of the funeral and that's it!"

Most pastors, I contend, neglect to take advantage of grief counseling. Sue is indicative of the said practice.

She shared, "No, I did not take advantage of grief counseling. I didn't think I needed it. I just put my head to the grindstone and persevered. I did have a wife of a colleague who is a trained counselor who contacted me and invited me several times informally to talk with her. She was so compassionate and understanding. I really appreciated her friendship during this time."

What appears to be the norm among clergy is opting out to take advantage of grief counseling. Sue's responses to the matters of participating in grief counseling for herself and/or referring bereaved church members were mixed. That is to say, the pastor declined to take advantage of grief counseling while referring bereaved families for such services. Also, she does not indicate referring clergy for affinity group counseling.

Pertinent to the Lingering Effects of the Death of Her Granddaughter

Three years passed since the death of Sue's granddaughter falls into the group of clergypersons, who do not take advantage of group counseling or being in an affinity group of ministers who lost loved ones. She informally participated in a group of grievers that leaned on each other as a support group. Sue did, however, recommend grief counseling to bereaved families of her congregation.

Dr. Shorb-Sterling candidly stated that she felt no immunity to pain, suffering, or grief due to her being a pastor. Further, she felt compelled to share her faith in the midst of her personal tragedy as a witness to her congregation.

There is not a day that goes by, she explained, when she does not speak to her granddaughter's pictures and mementos on a bookshelf in her family room.

Succinctly, Sue admitted that she manages grief through conversations about her granddaughter or something that triggers her memories. She said, "I love to talk about our granddaughter. I share memories with our family and encourage them to share memories. When something happens that I know she would have liked, I tell someone in the family, "Wouldn't she have loved this?"

Also, Sue turns to family members for help, those who truly understand the loss of their young family member. Dr. Shorb-Sterling remains open to the sharing of her emotions versus keeping them inside. She said, "When I was active clergy, I did express my emotions openly, sometimes with the entire congregation, especially shortly after the death, and periodically to trusted individuals within the congregation—particularly those who had experienced grief. They often would reach out to me. I had a couple who lost a baby. We often sat and talked about our grief, especially the grief of not experiencing the future with these children. In this way, those within the congregation who were grieving, and I, had a type of mutual ministry of grief sharing."

Sue shared what triggers her grieving moments, "Holidays, birthdays, particularly our granddaughter's birthday, Good Friday (the day of her death), family gatherings without her, watching my son's two daughters build a strong relationship as sisters, and then seeing my daughter's surviving daughter not have her big sister to be her companion and friend.

The performing of funeral services by Sue, especially for young people, proved difficult because of the death of her granddaughter complicated by COVID-19 restrictions. She commented, "Yes, from January 2020 through June 2020 I had thirteen funerals. This was about a year after my granddaughter's death. This was also at the beginning of the pandemic which made being with the dying person and their families difficult if not impossible. Many of these deaths happened to be leaders within the congregation. Grieving my own loss, COVID-19 restrictions, and preparing to retire made conducting these funerals almost impossible. I really had to dig down into the depths of my soul and rely on the power of God to get me through."

OBSERVATIONS

The Rev. Dr. Sue Shorb-Sterling, retired member, The Baltimore-Washington Conference, The United Methodist

Church, occupies a unique circumstance among clergy who grieve the loss of a loved one. Rev. Dr. Shorb-Sterling is a grandmother who suffered the loss of her ten-year-old granddaughter, due to a fatal disease.

The retired grandmother pastor opted not to respond to this writer's invitation to a person-to-person interview but agreed to answer a questionnaire submitted via email. She described her anticipatory grief because of her granddaughter's rapid health decline. Cognizant of the congregation's empathy for her loss, their questioning of why God allowed the death of the pastor's ten-year-old granddaughter, and especially during the Easter Season, Sue felt compelled to present a strong faith in God before her congregants.

Grief's impact upon Rev. Dr. Shorb-Sterling matched the level that her daughter and son-in-law experienced. She lived through the stages of grief such as denial, anger, depression, and finally acceptance. As a mother, she tried to be strong for her daughter and son-in-law while assuming her pastoral role. Her approach was not unlike others of us as pastors who try to work through their grief without the help of a grief counselor or therapist.

The retired pastor described her mixed feelings about the leadership within the judicatory. On the one-hand, the district superintendent appeared concerned about pastoral coverage for the Easter Service more than the well-being of the pastor. Yet, she received a personal call from the bishop who expressed sympathy on the loss of her granddaughter, described as a first in her twenty-three years of pastoral ministry.

Sue admitted to her public display of grief although not exhibited in her own church, but in her daughter's home church and during the Memorial Service at the Annual Conference. As mentioned, the retired pastor did not seek the help of a professional grief counselor; yet, without hesitation she referred congregants for such care.

Rev. Dr. Sue Shorb-Sterling, a retired pastor and grandmother, profiles the image of pastors who tend to maintain the persona of strength in the presence of their parishioners while dealing with their personal grief. She serves as an example of a clergyperson who is a grandparent suffering the same impact of grief as the parents of a child who has died; but has worked to camouflage that grief because she is clergy. She does not feel free to exhibit her pain. Moreover, it could be argued that taking advantage of professional grief counseling could have been beneficial.

Rev. Dorothea B. Stroman, The Aunt's Reflection

Rev. Stroman serves Clinton United Methodist Church, in the growing African American community of Clinton, Prince George's County, Maryland. During the late 1970s a demographic shift occurred as more African Americans moved into Clinton, MD. According to www.maryland-demographics.com, its largest racial/ethnic groups are Black (80.6%) followed by White (6.6%) and Hispanic (6.5%).

Clinton UMC, organized in 1965, was a predominantly White church at the time. Seven pastors served the congregation including Rev. Stroman who was the first woman and second African American clergyperson. She is in her eighteenth year of ministry at Clinton UMC!

Rev. Dorothea Stroman and her sister, Cynthia Gipson, widow of the late Rev. Joseph Gipson, shared a unique experience of loss. The Gipsons lost their son, who was Rev. Stroman's nephew. The loss of the young-adult nephew illustrates the impact upon a clergy family from multiple perspectives: At the time of the young man's death, Rev. Dorothea Stroman was (and still is) an active clergyperson serving a suburban church. The young man's father, Rev. Joseph Gipson, was alive. During the Celebration of Life, Rev. Gipson was so overwrought, he had to be helped out of the sanctuary. Alas, Rev. Gipson's passing occurred about a year later.

CYNTHIA GIPSON, THE WIDOW'S RESPONSES TO QUESTIONNAIRE

Cynthia Gipson gives the following description in her reaction to the news of her young-adult son's death, "I was at the hospital and family and friends were with me. God gave me a sign the night before my son's pronounced death that he was with Him. A calm came over me. However, one is not prepared to hear these words. I shed tears, [but] there was no loud outburst. I just felt empty."

The death of her son, Christopher, was due to a prolonged illness. She stated, "My son had a stroke at age eight. He developed Moya-Moya Disease (no functioning veins and arteries in the left hemisphere of his brain—only capillaries). He had a hemorrhagic stroke."

He died in 2009 when he was twenty-one years old. Christopher's father was seventy-three; his mother was fifty-nine at the time of their son's death.

Christopher joined his aunt, Rev. Dorothea Stroman's church, Clinton UMC and was active in its various ministries. According to his aunt, "the Conference and District Superintendent rallied around them."

His mother, Cynthia, contends, "[There was] disbelief and sadness [and they were] upset about how [some church members] treated him when he told them he didn't feel well." Because of Christopher's energetic activity with the various ministries in the church, some thought he was sloughing off.

Additional reactions to his death by others included sending condolences via correspondences, being present at the funeral service and participating on the program. The community of faith expressed its sympathy to the Gipson family.

Funeral preparations are emotionally and physically draining; Cynthia revealed, "I was on a sedative, and I had to make sure my son's needs and requests were met."

Not only was it difficult for her, but some of the pastors opted not to attend the services, according to them, "... because [the loss of Christopher] was like losing a family member and [they] didn't know what to say." Clearly, the loss of a colleague's child was problematic for them. So much so that they could not bring themselves to address the matter of confronting their own personal grief.

Cynthia Gipson, a Certified Lay Minister (CLM), responded to the question regarding taking time off after the death of her son, Christopher: "I am not a pastor. However, I went to a viewing of the oldest male member in the church who died a few days before my son. It took me two months before I returned to work because I had to care for other children with sickle cell disease. I wasn't sure how I would react when I saw his friends."

Grief counseling was beneficial to Christopher's mother, his aunt, Rev. Dorothea Stroman, an extended family member, and a friend. Mrs. Gipson commented: "I attended Compassionate Friends and Bereaved Parents of the USA. Even though I was a clergy spouse, no one suggested grief counseling. I googled groups for the loss of a child. I also took my sister, niece, and a friend of my son to a Compassionate Friend's meeting once a month. My family attended programs with Bereaved Parents of the U.S.A."

Rev. Stroman provided additional information about actions following the death of her nephew: "I attended *Compassionate Friends* with my sister for three or four years. [But] I did not take time off [to mourn]. Christopher was an organ donor. We attended a service for organ donor families. Christopher's name is on the wall at Bayview Hospital. For the past seventeen years, I have provided grief support ministry at my church."

Both Cynthia and her clergy sister, Dorothea, recommend grief counseling to bereaved families. Anecdotally, Christopher's mother continues to be in grief counseling after fourteen-plus years since his death.

***

The matter of Christians' immunity from suffering catastrophic and horrific occurrences in life is a subject biblically and theologically addressed in both the Old Testament and the Gospels. The narrative of Job in the Old Testament and Jesus' crucifixion in the Gospels, illustrate that Christians were subject to the devastations and the cruelties of life.

The Interpreter's Bible Commentary, Vol. IV, in the Reflections segment on Job 2:11-13, gave attention to the untenable belief of invulnerability from problems and stressors of life. It's stated, "... a theology that contains the unspoken assumption of a contract with God: God is bound to protect me from tragedy because I have been good or simply, I belong to God ... will not sustain a person in crisis; yet it is often thought subliminally in the way religious communities talk about God."

***

Cynthia answered, "Even though I am not a pastor, I have leadership roles in the church. It was important that I shared with others [about my experience] to help them through the grieving process."

Dorothea, her sister, succinctly stated, "No, I didn't feel immune as an aunt ... I just wasn't ready for Chris' [death].

Christopher's mother shares her thoughts about ongoing grief. "[I think about him] regularly. He is not with me physically, but his spirit is always with me." Both the mother and her clergy sister think about the young man often, and frequently talk about him.

In as much as grief is ongoing, Cynthia uses the following practices: "I pray, go through my emotions then continue with my son in my heart ... I grieve alone, but I will bring up his name with others so I can enjoy his memory...I honor his legacy ..." There are certain triggers, she said, that start her grieving moments: "Holidays, birthdays, blood drives, anniversary of death activities ..." Funeral services, especially for young people and children, are also difficult for Christopher's mother. Yet, she stated that sometimes she feels that way, "but I need to be there for the families."

She is a strong advocate for persons suffering with sickle cell. As a result, Cynthia devoted her energies on behalf of sickle cell families.

Pertinent to her deceased son's personal effects, Mrs. Gipson implied in her written response that she held on to the articles about her son because they served as comforting reminders of him. "It is comforting at times to remember that he [Christopher] lived. I don't want to forget." Also, both women agreed that Christopher came up regularly as part of their conversations, especially as they reflected on his love for children. However, such moments were also occasions of ambivalence due to the sadness because of his absence from them.

The theological understanding of God by both sisters has not changed. While Cynthia, the widowed clergy spouse, initially was angry with God but realized that her adult child's health deteriorated, her pastor-sister, on the other hand, looked forward to seeing her nephew again in eternity—with a gathering of the saints.

In summation, Cynthia stated, "God lends our children to us to care for. We are never ready for them to return to the Heavenly Father. It is up to us that our child(ren) lives a Christian life, a fulfilled [life]."

OBSERVATIONS

Certified Lay Minister Cynthia Belt-Gipson is the widow of the late Rev. Joseph Gipson. She is also the sister of Rev. Dr. Dorothea Belt-Stroman. Cynthia is the grieving mother of Christopher Gipson (a young adult) who died as a result of Moya-Moya Disease, which is connected to sickle cell. Cynthia's reaction to her son's death was not atypical of any other loving mother who lost her child because of a fatal disease. What distinguishes Certified Lay Minister Belt-Gipson is the action she took to confront the pain and sorrow caused by her child's death. She sought help from *Compassionate Friends*, an organization devoted to aiding parents who have lost children. Mrs. Belt-Gipson continues to be in affiliation after fourteen years subsequent to the death of her son.

The Rev. Dr. Dorothea Belt-Stroman is also the pastor of Clinton UMC, Clinton, MD. She shared along in her sister's grief. They journeyed together as they mourned. Both attended grief counseling and meetings with *Compassionate Friends*. However, Dorothea eventually ceased attending grief counseling sessions with *Compassionate Friends*. Rather, Pastor Dorothea Belt-Stroman established a grief counseling ministry at her church, where the ministry continues as of this writing.

The late Christopher Gipson's death affected his mother, Cynthia, his father (now deceased) and his aunt, Rev. Dorothea Stroman; and for the latter, it birthed a new ministry in Clinton UMC.

Christopher's mother and aunt exemplify the extent to which grief penetrates family structures.

CHAPTER SIX

When Clergy Grief Stems from Murder and Suicide

Rev. Dr. Bruce F. Haskins was an Elder with thirty-three years as full member of the Baltimore-Washington Conference, The United Methodist Church. His appointment was in the Baltimore Metropolitan District where he served the historic John Wesley United Methodist Church, located in the Walbrook Junction community in West Baltimore City. The church predominantly African American dates back to 1813. The congregation has been a staple in the community since 1959. During Dr. Haskins' tenure from 2011 until his death in 2016, the church registered 430 on its membership rolls while it enjoyed an average attendance of 138 per Sunday worship service.

Walbrook Junction according to Niche.com describes the community with a population of 3,066. This West Baltimore area offers an urban suburban atmosphere, while most of the residents rent their homes. The median income is $43,420. The residents with academic degrees list 4 percent master's, 9 percent bachelor's, and some with college and/or associate's 25 percent. High school graduates or those having equivalent are 50 percent. Persons having less than high school diploma are 12 percent.

The Haskins Family suffered unbearable grief with the violent death of their son Joseph and later the terminal illness of Bruce, husband, father, and grandfather. Dr. Deborah Haskins, widow and mother of her deceased son, Joseph, gave consent to this interview.

MY INTERVIEW WITH THE WIDOW OF THE LATE DR. BRUCE HASKINS

George: It is my hope that this study will shed some light on grief experienced by colleagues who lost children. Further, it will be a help now, and in the future, should such an event happen to other colleagues. Moreover, not only will the project be informative, but will be a comfort to other bereaved ministers, to let them know that they are not alone. Thank you so very much.

Deborah: You're welcome. Thank you.

George: I want to begin this session by getting some demographic data.

Deborah: Yes.

George: Your status is?

Deborah: I am the spouse of a deceased United Methodist clergy, Baltimore-Washington Conference. I am a retired Associate professor of counseling. I also am a professional counselor. I am licensed, I have my own consulting practice and counseling agency and practice. I'm basically semi-retired. Although, I'm retired full time from academia, I continue to do work in the field and share my gifts that God has given me, which includes a lot of community wellness trainings, as well as consultations as a content expert. That's who I am vocationally.

Personally, my family is very important to me and has always been. I'm a widow and have two children who are living, and sadly, one who's deceased. Then I have three grandchildren—young children.

George: To the best of your memory, what was the average worship attendance at this urban church?

[Dr. Haskins remembered the numbers a bit differently than actual documentation. One might say that she remembered with her heart and her head.]

Deborah: Let's see, the average, when we were there, I want to say, it might be approximately 300 or more. The church would be pretty packed. I'm just taking a guess.

I think it might have been even more than that. The church was always full. I want to say maybe 350 to 400 or more, on an average Sunday.

George: Okay, so this was a program-size church, because it was over 150.

[Arlin J. Rothauge offers the theory of congregational size in his booklet *Sizing Up a Congregation for New Members Ministry*. Family church: less than 50 active members; Pastoral church: 50 to 150 active members; Program church: 150 to 350 active members; and corporate church: 350 or more active members. Kevin E. Martin asserts in his *The Myth of the 200 Barrier: How to Lead Through Transitional Growth* that the program-size church is very different from a pastoral-size one. It is a staff-led, program driven community with high standards in all activities of the congregation ... have human-need ministries. pp 61, 65.]

Deborah: Yes. It was considered one of the anchor churches in the Baltimore-Washington Conference.

George: How many years did your husband serve in the Annual Conference?

Deborah: When he passed away ... Bruce passed away in January ... actually, Bruce had completed 30 years and was in his 31st year. Let me just do the math and see. Actually, our son passed away in ... he passed away in 2013. I remember this because they were planning a 30th year anniversary. He asked them to reschedule it because he of course, was not in the place of celebrating. That was in the summer of 2013, a couple of months after our son passed away. When Bruce passed away in 2016, he was in his 33rd year of ministry in the Baltimore-Washington Conference.

George: The first question—these questions will concern your initial grief and mourning responses. What was your knee-jerk reaction to the news of your child's death and how did your family react?

Deborah: The initial reaction was just shock. Just shock. [As a result of a home invasion, the homicide happened two streets from their residence at Joseph's best friend's house. Because of the close proximity of the crime, Deborah has not felt safe living there.]

We got the call 2:05 in the morning that said, "Please come quickly. Your son, Joseph, has been shot." They told us he was shot in the arm, in the shoulder and they said, "He's in surgery. You need to come quickly." When we got to the hospital and when I got in the car, we started praying immediately and my husband said, "Debby, please pray for my heart." I was going between praying for our son and praying for my husband's heart because he was a survivor of three heart attacks. When we got to the hospital, there was no time to call anybody. Our daughter was living in D.C. One thing Dr. DeFord ... there was no time to call anybody, and we got to the hospital ... we were praying, I was feeling like our son was going to be okay, because I felt like, *okay, they said he got shot. The bullet entered his shoulder*, and I'm thinking they're going to just get the bullet out, and I'm just praying that everything goes well.

We get there, the nurse comes to greet us and says, "Have a seat. I'm really sorry." She was very caring. "Your son is in surgery." I don't know if he honestly was still in surgery, if that's just what they tell you, but we're sitting there and I'm still feeling hopeful like, *okay. They're finishing surgery and they're going to come out and tell us that Jojo is going to be okay and we're going to be able to go in and see him.* Then the next thing I know, the nurse goes back in; then the next thing I know, the nurse comes out with the doctor.

The doctor introduced himself and said, "I'm sorry. You're the parents?"

"Yes, doctor. Dr. Haskins."

Then he just says, your son, Joseph, was shot. The bullet entered his shoulder, but it traveled through his lungs and his spine. [The doctor continued] "It severed his spine, and he was paralyzed. We worked hard and did everything we could, but we were unable to save your son."

At that point, I just collapsed on the ground. My husband is...we are both crying, and I'm screaming. My son—I remember Bruce just holding me and saying, 'Deb, we prayed. We asked God to take care of him. We prayed.' We just held each other. Then we were just in shock, just shock. Then we called my brother who lives in Pikesville, and my sister-in-law. Then we had to make a decision how we were going to get the information to our other two children. Our daughter lived in D.C.

My brother and my sister-in-law, who we had called, at some point while we were here waiting for the news, we did call them, and they came right away. I think my nephew is little, their son. At that time, he was probably like—I don't know—he's going into high school now, so he was still in elementary school. They had to wait for someone to come, their daughter to come, who was living not far. Then we call our nephew, who is their other child. He was living in Towson. He drove to DC because we did not want Joy [Dr. Haskins' daughter] to be alone when we called to give her the news.

When my nephew got there [Dr. Haskins called her daughter to say], "This is mommy and daddy. We're sorry. Please let your cousin in ... because we have something we need to share with you." Then she went and opened the door and let him in. Then when we told her, she collapsed. I have to protect my children. You know what I mean?

George: Yes.

Deborah: I guess I have to decide, maybe, I'm not going to be comfortable sharing all the details, but I will just say that our children were in shock just like we were. That was the initial—just disbelief and shock. Disbelief, shock, and anger, and confusion.

Then they let us go in and see ... After they cleaned our son, they let us see our baby boy, who was 6'8.5 feet tall. Dr. DeFord, to see our son, our baby, stretched out on that gurney, whatever you call it.

Oh ... he looked like he was just asleep. Then we were just clutching him and crying. It's just like a bad nightmare dream., like this isn't really happening. I just remember that part, it was hard to then leave our child. I just remembered that was very difficult. We didn't want to leave him, but we had to because then, the medical examiner's office is coming because it's homicide. Then we waited probably until that part was done, because we're not leaving our child alone at Sinai Hospital. Once that was done, we then came home. This was the day, Dr. DeFord, before Mother's Day.

He actually passed away the day before Mother's Day. Needless to say, Mother's Day will never be the same for me. The initial was shock, disbelief, confusion, anger, because now, there's a lot of questions that we don't even have answered. Now, we get home, and there's no time really, to begin to process anything because then, the detectives are here to question us and to share information. Then it was the whole process of contacting everybody. We called my mother, I think. She lives in South Carolina.

For her, it was the same thing, just total collapse, shock, disbelief, distraught. I think distraught is probably the better word. Just distraught. All of us, distraught. I will tell you; I don't know if this is the question or the next, what happened the next day for Bruce physically, because of the news.

George: Yes, you can include that.

Deborah: The next day, should I tell you that now?

George: Please.

Deborah: Okay. The next day, Bruce was on his way to tell his sister the news, who was disabled and dealing with chronic medical conditions—and Joseph [Dr. Haskins' now deceased son] had been his aunt's caregiver for almost a year. [Dr. Haskins' further explained that Bruce's cousin] was sitting in the car with him on the passenger side— [during the ride over, Bruce] he basically had two heart attacks.

George: My Lord!

Deborah: At the time, he didn't know, and [I] didn't know that either. He got to his sister's, which was just like a mile away, told her the news, and stayed there with her, just consoling her. I think he called and made sure somebody would come there to be with her.

Once he got home [Dr. Haskins explained how she and her husband, Bruce, were not sure just what to call the medical episodes he had experienced. Were they seizures or heart attacks?]

He was calling his doctor now so that he could get seen. They told him to come right away. [He saw his medical team at the University of Maryland.] When you have a defibrillator and pacemaker, they can look and track and see what happened. Sure enough, they looked at everything and he had a couple of heart attacks and that's what happened.

He couldn't drive for almost eight months. They limited him. He could not drive. That's what happened right away. That was the outcome of our son's death immediately.

George: What was his [Joseph] age at his death?

Deborah: He was only twenty years old. He would've been twenty-one that summer.

George: I can identify with you, particularly at the hospital, because I was with my son when he passed.

Deborah: Oh, wow, I'm so sorry. How old was your son, Dr. DeFord?

George: He was forty-two.

Deborah: Oh, bless your heart. I'm so sorry.

George: I recall those last several breaths. His circumstances were that he had a kidney transplant, and it was renal failure.

I shall never forget that day. It was May 28th at 4:15 a.m. at the University of Maryland Hospital, Room 6. I know what you went through. When they had to clean him up. I didn't want to let him go.

Deborah: Yes, absolutely. We know.

George: I know your pain. I know your pain.

Deborah: Yes. I know *your* pain, absolutely. We're in this together, we had no idea we'd be in this place.

George: Anyway. I walk the same journey with you, maybe different circumstances of transition.

Deborah: Sure.

George: This is what triggered me, too. It's just seared into your memory.

Deborah: Absolutely.

George: What was Bruce's age at the time of the death of your son, Joseph?

Deborah: Bruce hadn't turned fifty-three yet. He was fifty-two. [Bruce] was fifty-six when he passed away.

George: Moving from that, [clears throat] excuse me. Your child was buried [as opposed to cremation]?

Deborah: Yes.

George: Even though I think this was a question I should have asked earlier, but can you recall your congregation's reaction upon the awareness of the loss of your child?

Deborah: Yes. They were in despair and in shock, disbelief, compassionate, very sad. They felt the trauma, too, because this was, one, a death of a child, but also, a homicidal death. People were angry, the congregation. I just remember, there was a tremendous amount of love, compassion and support, but also, I would have to say that there was also—which is typically what happens in the world, but also Christians, too ... [She veered off in thought] There was a lot of spiritual support, but at the same time— what I don't like is ... [She appeared to be careful with her words] ... it wasn't that they didn't mean well, but I just think that humans struggle, when they start to share what I call prescriptives.

He's in a better place. God wanted him more. God loved him first. He was God's, nobody owns ... He didn't belong to us. All of those things [those prescriptives] don't help the parents, who are struggling, just in general, with the death of their child and the death of anyone, to be honest. It was a lot of that, too. I think people struggle with just being silent and just not saying anything or just letting you know, 'I'm here and supporting you and loving you,' [a ministry of presence] There was a lot of support like that.

I think also, because it was homicide too—Even if it wasn't a homicidal death, people want to know more information. They wanted to know what happened. I don't think that most people even got access to us, to be honest, because the church, our associate pastor, and the armor-bearer, who is the head of the bereaved ministry, the pastoral care ministry, who is trained as a pastoral counselor and has a degree from the program I got my PhD from, they pretty much protected us.

George: Good.

Deborah: And didn't give access to. For example, because we live not far from the church, we live in our home, people just descending on the home because that would've just worn us out. We couldn't tolerate that. That was just too much. My husband's family ... he has a large family, then I have a large family on my father's side, but just his family alone, there's a lot of people, so every day there was a lot of people here. But the congregation pretty much did—I think they asked what we wanted and what would help us the most—they basically protected our hearts and our spirits immediately. That was immediate.

Then I can tell you a little bit more of what happened when we returned to the church in terms of when Bruce returned to worship, and we started attending worship again.

George: How much time did you take off?

Deborah: I took off—I started to go back in July. He had passed away in June. Maybe not even July. I think I didn't go back actually, until August. I was at the time, the department chair of three graduate programs, and I was at the time, leading two program accreditations, and I was also on a tenure track. I was in year three of a six-year tenure track. I also was teaching. At the time he was killed, I had just started teaching, or I was about to start teaching a course that summer, and then my load is two courses in the fall and spring. Because I was paralyzed emotionally, I could not go back to work right away.

They immediately took my classes and gave them to someone else to cover. Then they had to just cover the program because I was incapable of doing anything. I don't think I went back until maybe the end of July, August. What happened was I remember I got to a point; it might have been July [when] I had to get out of the house. I just couldn't be here anymore. I felt like I was going to suffocate. Part of it was, every minute, I was waiting for our son to come flying through the door because that's what he used to do. He would say, 'Hey, mom. Hey dad.'

I remember driving to campus, which was in DC and the whole time I'm driving, I'm on 695, I'm feeling like, *I can't do this, I can't do this.* Then I got on 295, the whole time, I'm feeling, *I can't do this. I want to turn back around.* I got to campus; I just remember feeling like I was going to throw up. I felt sick. I also had a lot of anxiety. Because I felt afraid, I didn't want to talk about it. The other part of it was I felt exposed. I felt so vulnerable. I felt stripped. I felt emotionally stripped and I didn't know if I was going to be able to function as the director of [three graduate programs and being the lead of two program accreditations], I had a lot of responsibilities.

I got there, but I had a conversation with my dean who wanted to know, everybody was really upset, everybody was traumatized. They had to go and explain what happened to students. The students were traumatized and very sad about it and sad for us, and there was a lot of compassion at the university, but I had to tell my dean when she asked me, 'what could people do?' They wanted to know how they could best support me. I told them that when I come back to work, what I needed was I needed people not to ask me what happened. I could not talk about it at work.

I knew I needed to be able to compartmentalize. And when I'm at [the university], as difficult as it's going to be, I need to be able to focus and work. It was just too emotionally overwhelming for me to talk about, but I just remember, once I got there and people were glad to see me, and there was a lot of hugging and support, they bought me a big wicker basket that my colleague, the most senior person, had put together, and each of them had put self-care gifts in there for me.

I just broke down and cried, Dr. DeFord. I just broke down and cried because there was so much love and care that despite us feeling like the world took away our son and there was so much evil, I felt the love with so many others. I only stayed for an hour. Then the next week, I could only do two hours.

I tell you, I had to slowly build up until I got to seven hours. That took over maybe a two-month period. By September, when the university needed to cover my classes, then I was back unfortunately, in full force. Now, let me just say this. When I look back at that, I really should have gone out on disability, short-term. I should not have gone back to work because the nature of my work is very intense. I'm a counselor-educator, I'm teaching about counseling and I'm hearing cases of trauma, which include homicidal loss. I'm a clinical supervisor of the students when they're in practice, on an internship, so I'm being triggered around the clock.

That was one of the questions I had, 'How can I return to the classroom?' I got support over that, but when I look back at it, I really feel like I should have gone out on short-term disability. I really should have—because I was impaired. I was impaired emotionally.

Now, I'll tell you when Bruce went back [to the pulpit]. And I'll never forget. His first Sunday back was Father's Day.

George: My goodness!

Deborah: Let me just say this, I was scared to death, Dr. DeFord. I asked my husband, 'Are you sure this is something you can do?' Concerned for him, I actually was afraid that he was going to have another heart attack. [As the time to return to his senior pastor duties drew near] he realized he wasn't emotionally ready. He talked to the DS and the folks. Then he waited until September to go back. At that point, he was basically on—I don't think it was like a formal disability leave, but—he was basically on leave. That would've been like June, July, August, like four months later.

George: That was sabbath leave.

Deborah: He did try to go back. Yes, he tried to go back like a month later and that was too much. Actually, one of the things I'd like to work on is a project of Bruce's sermons. If I ever do, that's going to be the next to the last sermon. The last sermon is going to be the one he wrote on his cell phone while he was in cardiac ICU for that year. Anyway, that's what happened.

George: What response did you receive from the district and/or conference leadership?

Deborah: Total support, we had a tremendous support from the bishop and the DSs, all his colleagues, nothing but support. It was just such an outpouring. I think that at Joseph's viewing there must have been a thousand people that came up. For his service, the church was packed like never before. The church was packed all the way to the community room. People couldn't even get in. There was so much support we had from the conference.

Cards, prayers, people stepping in to fill a gap for him in terms of pulpit supply, and funerals and anything else that was going on. The associate pastor had to step up, Pastor

Prioleau, I love her. She was our associate pastor, and she has been our pastor. Honestly, she's still my pastor today.

George: Now, what about the matter of grief counseling, and how long was the counseling?

Deborah: I asked my husband if we could go into grief counseling because my husband was a person who believed God was his therapist. I think over the course of the marriage I finally had worked on him enough that he really understood that mental health counseling and therapy could be really helpful. He was able to, as a pastor, recommend it. But he didn't necessarily [take advantage of therapy] for himself, ever. He never accessed therapy for himself. While I did and I'm comfortable in sharing it because I believe in therapy, I'm a therapist. I talked to my husband and our children about therapy.

I shared with my husband. I asked him if we could go [into therapy] because I felt like we needed to be able to get support together. Because we are parents of a child [she asserted] who died and who was murdered. They say that a lot of times marriages don't survive the death of a child, and we made a commitment that that wasn't going to be us. We actually talked about that. We said that that was not going to be us. My husband said, "I am open to it." I was so hopeful. Then we had to figure out who, because I'm a counselor educator. I was a formal director of clinical training.

One of the big challenges was trying to find who we could trust. What was our preferences for counseling and who could we trust because he was a pastor in an urban church? I was a counselor educator that had worked at a university for some time where I know clinicians and I didn't want to trust my story, my heart, and spirit with just anybody. We wanted to protect [our privacy]. [And] we didn't think we wanted to go into a group because we just didn't feel like we would have anonymity in the same way.

Even though people are trying to convince me otherwise, I know as a counselor educator, when you are having a training, you're going to be presenting cases with other people. I didn't want my family being presented in some case conference. I had taken a little time and we did find a therapist with Stella Maris Counseling Center who was amazing. She was just so wonderful and that's who we started to see. In the meantime, I just also have to say that we didn't just lose our son, but as you know we lost our nephew a year later to homicide. We helped his mom as part of the village. I'm saying the family village raised him because his father died when he was only eighteen months old. He grew up like a brother-cousin to our children. He was murdered a year after Joseph.

He never really recovered. That's when he was hospitalized. He was on life support for six weeks. Then, the whole medical crisis and trauma for a year until God took him home to heaven.

That's the impact of losing our child and losing our nephew.

George: Let me go back to the point about going for grief counseling. I think, maybe not so much in the words that you've used, many clergy, when they suffer such an experience as losing a child—I would say that they resist going to counseling. Not that I negate the effectiveness of prayer, but I use the expression, "We stuff it under our robe and go on." [The ancient Roman poet, Ovid, said, 'Suppressed grief suffocates; it rages within the breasts, and is forced to multiply its strength.']

Deborah: Yes, that's deep. Yes. Because we're supposed to be so spiritually and faithfully strong, it's almost like, "You've got your faith and you are such a strong spiritual leader, you're going to be okay." People don't realize you're human just like everybody else. You're no different than any person. Sometimes every clergy person believes that they really are going to be okay, even though they don't feel like they can start to—it's almost like you can convince yourself that that's what you are able to do.

George: I guess there's a sense that we're immune to these situations because of who we are and whose we are but that's not the case, and that's my argument. I often think in terms of the counseling aspect. I don't know if you are familiar with Paul C. Rosenblatt and Beverly R. Wallace's *African American Grief*. It was done back in the early 2000s. It reads, "One difference from Euro-Americans was that some people wanted an African-American therapist or valued being in a support group with other African-Americans."

165

There was, for some, a sense that the life experience of African Americans and the personal family and community issues of loss were much easier to deal with in a relationship with an African American professional or among other grieving African Americans. Coming back to clergy, I think that if members of clergy were in an affinity counseling group, such would be more beneficial. In fact, this was one of the questions I had—if you recommended clergy, who suffered the loss of a loved one, to participate in the grief counseling for clergy only?

Deborah: Yes. I think it would be very beneficial because I think that one of the challenges is that the issues [and experiences] that clergy face, and the clergy family, are very unique and different, and not the same.

[She recalled something her husband, Bruce, stated]. When Joseph was killed, I remember him saying, when we were in therapy with the grief counselor, 'Do I really believe what I have been teaching and preaching for all these years now with the death and the murder of our child and then when our nephew was murdered?'

I think that clergy could find a lot of support and encouragement and hope if they were able to participate in a group with other persons like themselves who really understand the struggle. Also, like my husband used to say, whenever I was very concerned about his health and [wanting him] to take some time off, he would say, 'The congregation wants you to take time off, until you take time off.' Okay?

That's what he would say. They're all for you taking time off until you actually take the time off. There's actually a double-edged message. It's like, 'We really want you to be committed to your self-care, pastor, but don't take too much time with it. We still want you to come see about me.' My husband used to say this, 'People die when you go on vacation.' [Laughs]

Then you get the call. 'Pastor someone so and so, my loved one passed away, but we only want you to celebrate, do their eulogy.' Prior to COVID, now, you get a couple of weeks, so you could go on vacation now because the way it is with COVID, sometimes it's going to take a couple of weeks to bury your loved one. Then you're stuck with, you got to now take care of somebody else instead of taking care of your needs and your family.

That, I feel like a grief group for clergy could be really helpful. I think the challenge though is going to be this, because my husband used to say this, too. One time I asked him, this was years ago when he started having health challenges, I asked, "Who do you talk to when you are struggling?"

He said, 'I talk to God, and *then* I talk to you.'

Then, of course, he has his small circle of people he could trust, his best friends. I said, "But what if you need to talk to somebody about me? You still need to have somebody to go to, but what if you have someone to go in ministry?"

He's like, 'Well, I can't really talk to other clergy.'

I'm like, "Why not?"

He said, 'Because they're struggling just like me, and I don't want to burden them.'

That's what my husband said. I remember that. He said, 'I don't want to burden them anymore with my stuff. They got a lot that they're doing. I don't want to have to add to that burden.'

That's what he told me Dr. DeFord. I thought, *how sad is that?* I said [to him], "How sad is that that as a clergy person, that you can't necessarily get support by your peers because you don't want to add to be their burden, like how you interpret it, and you're going to weigh them down with more stress because you're passing on."

Then the other thing too is, you might be concerned about if the conference becomes aware or they think you're not strong or emotionally or whatever, is that going to impact your ministry opportunities? I think that question is similar to what probably why I went back to work so quickly because I was on a tenure track. If I didn't finish the tenure, I don't have a job.

George: I think you're exactly right in that assumption. Many of the clergy, particularly within the United Methodist community, some may feel a bit paranoid that is I share this, this would be ammunition used against me. That's why I used the expression, we just stuff it underneath of our robes and go on.

Did you feel immune to such an unforeseen or horrific evident due to one's calling as a pastor and the death of your son? How do you think of your deceased children and what do you do to manage your grief?

Deborah: This is what I tell people, and this was very evident to me. I thought that homicide happened to other people until it happened to us, so I really did feel immune. Honestly, I felt like if you live your life as a good person, which we were trying to do, we take care of so many people in the world, we're doing such good in the world for God, I really believe that harm would not come to us.

When our son was murdered, it forever altered my perspective of the world. It changed how I viewed the world now, and it helped me to see, yes, there's really sin in the world and there are evil people in the world. For me to think that my family is so special and different, and I am, I must've been in la-la land. That's what I experienced. It altered forever my view of the world and who we really are.

George: How often do you think of your deceased child or children and in your case, husband, what do you do to help manage your grief?

Deborah: I think about them all the time, every day, 24/7. If you're coming to my house, you're going to be surrounded with their pictures. I say that because I remember when my best friend died when I was twenty-three, that was my first major emotional death that impacted me. I remember a friend telling me, 'Why do you still have her pictures up? You need to put these away, this is going to make you feel worse.' I thought that was the craziest thing I've ever heard of. Back then, that's what you did. Now, I told him, 'I don't care. If you care, if you come into my house, you may be uncomfortable because you're going to see pictures everywhere.'

I have a picture of my husband and our son on my dashboard in my car. I have him in my locket on my chest. What I do to help get through, what's a big part of it, was therapy, grief counseling. I went to a fifteen-week grief counseling group through March Funeral Home [and then through], Roberta's House which is amazing. I think it was maybe the summer after my husband passed away or a year because it's foggy to me right now. I really didn't want to participate, Dr. DeFord. Annette March convinced me to. She's one of Mr. and Mrs. March's children who's the head of the Roberta's House who started it all.

I resigned from [The Hope program for the Baltimore Conference.] when our son was murdered. I couldn't do it. I told the bishop and the DS [district superintendent] overseeing it, "I can't help other people deal with their losses right now, I need to focus on my family."

The first therapist, we actually stopped seeing because the therapist was too behavioral and my husband felt really angry that the therapist wasn't letting me share my anger and asked this crazy question: 'Can you tell me, let's look at what are some of the positives that have come out resulted from Joseph's death?' Can you believe he asked me that—

and we're like, *what in the world are you talking about, positives?*

I said, there is nothing positive from our son's death. There is nothing positive that comes out of murder. *What are you talking about?* My husband said, he wasn't going back to see this therapist. We found another therapist instead, and she was incredibly just a gift, but I say all that to say about therapy, it helped us to breathe basically because I told people when your child is killed or when your child dies, it's hard to breathe. It's hard to breathe, and I told people this, your children are your breath, and when they die, it is hard to breathe. That's what I told people.

[Tracie Miles, in her meditation, *Encouragement for Today*, on crosscards.com, Feb. 11, 2022, she says, 'My grief had been suffocatingly heavy, but over time, just as He promises, God truly turned my sorrow into joy.']

That's the first thing that came to me because I started hyperventilating and my girlfriend, who's a nurse, the next day when I couldn't even, I was like in shock and I going through all of just the overwhelming despair, and I couldn't breathe. And my girlfriend who's a nurse kept telling me, just breathe, slow breath. She helped me to breathe.

She took care of me physically, and I had to be on medication because it was just awful, and so the therapy has helped do the rebuilding. It has also been helpful in the questioning, emotionally and spiritually, the questions that we have to God are like, *how could this awful thing happen? Why didn't we go first? Why did our son have to die? He was a parent of a two-month-old. Why is our granddaughter without her father and why is it that one day I'm going to be stuck with having to have the conversation with her about what happened to her father?* The therapy is helping with all of that process.

[What she's asking and stating are issues related to theodicy. As mentioned earlier, theodicy is interpreted as God allowing or permitting evil to exist in spite of God's omnipotence.]

The therapy is helping us, [it] helped us be able to sort through some very painful and difficult emotions and thoughts, and then also experiences in the world because this is what happens as you know, the world is only going to give you a couple of weeks. If you're lucky, the world might give you a month. If it's a good week, you might be lucky to get thirty days, but then at a certain point, the world's going to be saying, *okay, your son has passed away, but you now have to move on* and then it's going to be saying to you, *your son would want this.*

They tell you some crazy things. I'm never saying [those things] to people like, *it's time to move on.* You have to live all those things that people say, while you are still bleeding. You can't breathe. You're suffocating. You can't even breathe, and people are telling you to move on. So, the therapy, actually … first of all … my faith in God … *that* gives me hope in the world to focus on not just evil, but that there is a lot of love and there are good people in the world. That's what God has helped me to be able to see.

[Elizabeth Kubler-Ross & David Kessler in their work, *On Grief & Grieving*, contend, "Most corporations allow three to five days of bereavement. Very few, if any, will say, 'Take as much time as you need' We may go back physically but not necessarily mentally... If you do not take the time to grieve, you cannot find a future in which loss is remembered and honored without pain."]

God, my journey with Jesus Christ and the Holy Spirit helps me to take one day at a time, one breath at a time, one thought at a time and to be restored. But then the therapy is helping me to also breathe emotionally and physically. And then I also exercise daily. Because I got to get out of me—all of that stuff staying in my body. It is trauma and trauma stays in your body.

George: That's toxic, too.

Deborah: Exactly, it's toxic. So, I have to like, I'm a walker daily. I walk like two to three miles, and I do that because it helps move things around and to get it out of my body. But I also find meaning, and I'm grateful, that our son had a daughter and that I see him in her. I'm able to still be present so that I can show up in her life and her brother's life. They give me hope in the world.

When I see them, it gives me more of a will to keep living. They bring me joy, our children, Jason and Joy, bring me joy and my grandkids and my family and my friendship village, which includes my ministry village. All of those tools for me have helped, and helped Bruce, also to keep breathing. And all this took quite a while because the first couple of years, especially, were very dark.

I really isolated both of us. I told people I didn't want to be around people. Just the first year, especially, people, weren't around both of us. We just didn't, couldn't tolerate too much contact with family or friends. We spent a lot of time together as a couple, we spent a lot of our time just taking care of each other, supporting each other, supporting our children and our daughter-in-law and our grandkids. So, we worked as a team to make sure that they were going to make it. And so, I feel more joy today. But now this is seven years later.

It took the first five years before I could really have that cloak of darkness not covering me so completely. I don't even know if I could put a point on it. I would say, now, in year seven, since I've been retired for two years, and the reason I retired was because I needed to focus on my wellbeing, I just got to a point [where] I became emotionally burnt out.

George: Let me ask you this question: Was it difficult for Bruce to do funerals for young people after the death of your son?

Deborah: Yes. Those were always not easy which I'm sure you would agree to. I'm trying to remember if he had any after Joseph. I'm not even sure, to be honest, if he did. I don't know that I could recall if he ended up doing any at John Wesley or anything.

I will say this; my nephew died a year later, and Bruce got so sick that he couldn't even go to our nephew's homegoing service. He was immobile. Everyone was very concerned, and I was texting him the whole time. I really didn't want to leave him, he insisted that we leave. He didn't want us to stay at the house and miss it.

That's just I guess an example of how difficult it was. Well, our daughter is three years older than her brother, so my nephew was actually two years older than Joseph. It was very hard; it was very hard. My heart broke. Like I said, and then he [Bruce] went to cardiac arrest almost six weeks later.

George: What advice would you give to other clergy regarding the death of their children?

Deborah: I think the first advice that I would give is to recognize that at this point you are not a clergy person. You're a pastoral leader, you are human. You are a human being who has suffered a loss and you deserve the same support and opportunity to grieve just like anybody else. No more, no less, you deserve to have whatever you need to help you and your family work through this—begin and continue through this grief journey for however long it takes.

[And] Not to hold yourself up as this pastoral leader that's supposed to be able to get through this, too, no matter how faithful we are and how much you're a man or woman of God. I think that would be number one. Recognize your vulnerability, and that you deserve the same level of care and support and time as any person. Then the second thing is, I would recommend that they actually participate in grief support. Even if it's not for a long time. 'It's helpful,' as one of my girlfriends said to me as a psychologist.

'I like going to therapy because now I have somebody who can care for me.' That's what she told me, some years ago. I really think that that is important for clergy and their families. Let somebody care for you for a change. You don't have to be the one always caring for somebody, let somebody else be in a position of caring for your heart, your spirit, your physical self, and all of you. That's the second thing. Then the third, I guess, I would say, is that losing your child or someone who's close to you, it's going to also mean that, as a child of God, we're going to need to process the impact of [such loss] on our own faith identity and who we are with God.

We need time also to journey through that. There's no timetable. I'm still struggling with the questions.

[Deborah reflected on the deaths of her loved ones.] I was like, this is crap. This is crappy that our son isn't here. This is crappy. This is really crappy. I don't understand *that* God. I still need help with that. I need you to explain to me why our son is not here and why our nephew and why my husband ...? I don't get it. I still need to talk to God about that. I may not get those answers here on earth. It may be in heaven, where it all becomes clear, but I still need to raise the questions when I feel it.

I don't want anybody telling me that I don't have the right to ask that question. I don't need people telling me that

you need to have more faith or that God would want you ...,
or Bruce would even want you .... You know what, I've heard
that.

I need you to know that my faith in God is strong, but
our son was murdered, my nephew was murdered. And my
husband—they murdered his heart. I'm going to be raising
these questions. This is not an indicator of being less
faithful, but we have the right to be able to express whatever
your heart cries and whatever it's trying to express. I don't
need anybody to evaluate it and I don't need anyone to judge
it.

Then the other thing that goes along with this, Dr.
DeFord, is I don't want people to try to manage my grief.
That's really what the whole matter is. The number three:
don't try to manage it yourself and don't let anybody else
manage it.

George: Has your theological understanding about God
changed since the death of your son, nephew, and husband?
Do you feel anger toward God for not exempting you from
the anguish of the death of your child or husband? Also,
have you removed any personal belongings or memorabilia
of your child and how difficult was it to remove the items
and what have you kept?

Deborah: That's a really good question. It's funny you
asked that because even just this week, I was faced with that.
Sometime in that first year, I started going through Joseph's
clothes and packing them up and asking his brother what he
wanted, asking his sister what she wanted to keep. She

wanted one of his coats or jackets, for example. [Deborah mentioned that even though Joseph was living on his own, in their home, she'd kept his bedroom intact.] I had the room repainted a few months after his murder that summer. My sister actually painted it for us, and my girlfriend helped with the baseboards because my sister couldn't do it. My girlfriend came and did that for us.

He was a basketball player and so he had really meaningful memorabilia—his jerseys from the teams he played on, different memorabilia from Carmelo Anthony, [basketball player for the Los Angeles Lakers], things like that. What I have done is I've put all of that in a bin so that when his daughter gets to be of an age where she can really appreciate it, then I'm going to be giving those to her. [Because they love basketball], I also gave his stepsons items that belonged to their stepdad. I gave away one of Joseph's Dwayne Wade jerseys. [Dwayne Wade, former basketball player for Miami Heat].

I have a picture of Carmelo Anthony that I'm going to have reframed that was Joseph's. I'm going to give that to our grandson when he turns 15, the end of October. [2021].

I still have some of his things though, his clothing, et cetera, but I'm not able to give everything away. And that has to be okay. I'm not going to force myself to do it because I feel like, I guess, there's a part of me that almost feels like when I give those things away, I'm giving *him* away. That's when I'm accepting that our son is no longer alive, and I can't do that. He's still alive to us; he's still alive to our daughter. He's still here and I can't just pack everything up as if he's no longer here.

Some people would look at that and say, 'Well, you're just limiting your grief.' This is what I say to them, "It's my grief. It's not anybody else's to control." I'm not going to have somebody tell me what I need to do. I tell people, "Don't let other people tell you to go and pack everything up." Everybody is different. Some people need to do that, but I don't need that. That doesn't work for me.

Dr. DeFord, even though my husband, as faithful as he was, with his faith in God, and he may have been ready, he struggled. He struggled with our son's death. When my husband was struggling during his transition time, the Holy Spirit took over and I grabbed my husband's face and I prayed him through heaven. Even in his fight for his life, in his despair of losing our son, he still was struggling.

That's it for parents who you lost your child or someone who you love so deeply it is painful, it's heartbreaking, it takes your breath away, and no matter how faithful we are, it's still difficult. My husband was, as you know, like you, a man totally committed to God. A child of God, man, and woman, totally committed to God in Jesus Christ and had the Holy Spirit all through him, but we still struggle. It doesn't matter, we are no different with the struggle.

[Her son,] Joseph gave me a vase that I have in the kitchen. I'm looking at it right now. He and his fiancée gave it to me, I think, for Mother's Day or something. [It] has died and it's one of those sturdier plants. It's just a little stem of it now. There's no life on it, but it is hanging in my window, and I will probably still have it there until the day I go to heaven.

I don't plan on getting rid of it, so I understand what you're saying, and that really is a really great question to ask. I definitely have—I'm trying to think. I used to sleep with his picture of the funeral program for probably the first two years. Of course, it got weathered away. I have his pictures right there, all in my room. Again, I used to hold his picture when I would fall asleep. I was holding his picture. Those are very important for us. I think it's very helpful and healing for us, so thank you for asking that question.

I pray that [people] will be educated to understand that clergy needs a lot of support also and that they give them the time and the resources that they need to heal in the best way. And that they don't participate in a dynamic like the world can, where you have a certain timeframe, but you just are expected to move on. [This is also an expectation of congregations.]

Just recognizing that it is a journey and that on the journey, sometimes you move ahead like they told us when Bruce was in ICU, two steps forward, one step back, two steps forward, and one step back. That's sometimes how the journey can be. It's not anything wrong with the person, it's just, this is part of healing. We need to recognize that and provide people the support that they need to do it in the time that they need.

Then also, I guess, recognizing the cultural differences and the gender differences and particularly men, I feel, because they don't have the cultural support in the world. [The general thinking is that] men are supposed to be able to be even stronger but it's not that easy.

George: Again, according to O'Hara, in her book, *A Grief Like No Other*, she mentions, "Grieving does not exempt us from the standard gender roles." Men generally grieve differently than do women. In our culture, men are taught not to show their emotions. Historically, women are the ones who are encouraged to openly grieve while men are supposed to be the pillars of strength. For male clergy, we stuff it in our robes and keep going and don't show our emotions. However, there are times when you have to be emotive; I believe.

Deborah: Exactly!

George: There was a value in the ancient times to have had paid mourners. In our family, at least on my wife's side, it was jokingly mentioned about a dear aunt of ours: you knew at every funeral, Aunt Romaine was going to make a scene (crying and wailing). It got to a point that some of the family members would clock to see when she would go off during the funeral service.

Aunt Romaine's behavior, in a sense, was cathartic. It happened because there was the expectation, she was going to do it. Rather than sadness, there was a moment of humor and release. Then that becomes part of the family history and jokes.

Deborah: I can relate to that. Yes, thank you. Let me tell you. I think I told you—any image of pastors' wives or clergy spouses of the ministers' family [are expected to show that they] have it all together. That went out the window when our son was killed. I didn't care. I was snotting and crying every Sunday. I was screaming. It was very bad. Then I would feel guilty. I felt exposed. Then I felt really—I don't know what the word is, exposed and vulnerable. Then I felt like even a degree of shame, almost. Like I'm not supposed to do that. What are people going to think about me? I had to go through all of that. I really couldn't control it. It just happened. The more I needed it to come out ... and it came out in the place where I feel safe which was in worship.

I had to let go of that. It still didn't make it easy for me. What the church did, I'll just tell you this, they sent someone, one of the armor-bearers, to sit with me. She would console me and support me. I'm very close to this one. She's a sweetheart. I love her. She never asked me questions. She just would sit there and hold my hand or just hug me because my husband couldn't come and console. He was in the pulpit.

One thing that I'm grateful for is that he didn't get so worried. As if *not* to say, like, 'Well, you got to stop doing that.' He never said that to me. I'm so grateful because some people when you're in ministry, they have this expectation of how you're supposed to present yourself. I felt that. My husband didn't, but I felt that.

He was like, 'Listen, ministry families are no different than anybody else's family. Okay? We have challenges, too.' I felt really exposed. I felt like, *What are people going to say? What are they going to think?* Then, the Lord had to help me with that, Dr. DeFord. The Lord had to just basically say, 'Okay, you have no control over this. As you can see, you need just to come out. I'm going to help you with this.'

I'm grateful that I am comfortable in my own skin, and emotionally mature enough that I could let that go. To say, "Okay, I don't care what anybody thinks." If anybody has something to say about it, then please don't come over here and say it because I really don't care. If you do say the wrong thing, then you're going to hear about it. You're may hear about it from me, and you're going to probably hear about it from my husband, too. I think it also hopefully helps people to know—What I hope is that people would be able to free themselves, too, because we especially as Black people—we are so strong. All that is true, but it can also be a burden for us.

George: The funeral service and celebration of life service is also a means of serving as a catharsis for the people in that the celebrated part and opportunity to release.

I attended a funeral service in one of our African brother's churches. They had the singing and praying band come from Magothy, Maryland. In the performance of their part of the worship service, the African pastor got up from his seat in the pulpit and danced. As the members of the singing and praying band danced, the pastor said, "I feel like I'm back at home,' because of the expressiveness of the people and, also, the persons that were singing and praying in the band."

I think sometimes we suppress our innate feelings because we have been so influenced by the majority culture and tend to mimic them. Inwardly, we want to be expressive.

Deborah: Yes. That's true. I probably gave you too much.

George: No. This was good. You have been very helpful. May I have a brief prayer with you?

Deborah: Oh, thank you so much. Thank you.

George: [Prayer] Gracious God, thank you for this time of personal sharing and reflecting over loved ones who transitioned from this realm into the realm of eternal life.

Thank You, God, for Joseph and your servant Bruce Haskins, as they stood taller among men and in their own unique ways ministered to your people.

Thank You, God, for your servant Dr. Deborah Haskins, mother, wife, and servant of thine while she continues to grieve and mourn the loss of her son, Joseph, and husband, Bruce, lest we do not forget her nephew, Reuben.

God, *You*, know what it was like to lose Your Son, Jesus the Christ, and the victory of the resurrection.

Bless your servant Dr. Deborah Haskins and her family, children, and grandchildren.

Amen.

OBSERVATIONS

Dr. Deborah Haskins, counselor-educator, and spouse of a pastor who served a church that was the staple in an urban community, gave an account of unimaginable loss of her son, Joseph, nephew, and lastly her husband, Bruce. The triadic deaths occurred within a span of three years. Joseph and his cousin died as result of violence while her husband Bruce suffered complications with his heart condition, exacerbated by the deaths of his son and nephew.

Prior to her clergy husband's death, the Haskins sought grief counseling. Deborah averred that her husband wanted to receive his counseling from her; however, because she, too, grieved, it was necessary for them to have a counselor who was objective and a non-family member. Their initial experience with a therapist, she mentioned who was neither of their ethnicity nor culture, was not positive; therefore, they sought another grief counselor who met their needs.

Dr. Haskins is matter of fact about her emotional state and her reliance upon her faith in God. The trauma of hearing the attending physician's explanation as to why her son was unable to survive the gunshot wound to his body, their futile efforts to save him, resulted in her uncontrolled and unrestrained open grief. Further, during the funeral service, her unrelenting grief and mourning continued.

Mrs. Haskins' public grieving and mourning was beneficial. The ancient Roman poet Ovid said, "Suppressed grief suffocates, it rages within the breast, and is forced to multiply its strength." Grief if suppressed will cause physical consequences to a person's health and well-being, such as anger, depression, shortness of breath, to name a few. King David, the psalmist, wrote: "When the righteous cry for help, the Lord hears, and rescues them from all their troubles. The Lord is near to the brokenhearted and saves the crushed in spirit." (Psalm 34:17-18). And in another psalm, 'Be gracious to me, O Lord; for I am in distress; my eye wastes away with grief, my soul and body also. For my life is spent with sorrow, and my years with sighing; my strength fails because of my misery, and my bones waste away,' said David. (Psalm 31:9, 10). The value of expressing one's grief and mourning is cathartic.

The giving away of personal items of a deceased loved one exacerbates the pain of loss; for the wife of the late Rev. Dr. Bruce Haskins and mother of Joseph (Jojo), the tangibles served as a means of filling the lacuna created by their deaths. Both husband and child seemed to be still alive.

Dr. Haskins found herself in a unique sisterhood of widows of late pastors who had the daunting task of removing the personal effects of their late husbands. Mrs. Beverly M. said, "... I had no idea how difficult it would be to dispose of his belongings. How could I give away or throw away things that belonged to him without feeling that I was removing him from my life. I have spent many moments in prayer asking God for the strength to handle this overwhelming heartbreaking task ... it is the more personal things that caused and are still causing me grief ... doing this only enables me to postpone the inevitable. In reading how others dealt with this, someone said, 'The only thing more painful than seeing your loved one's items every day is seeing them in the trash ... I keep a few that are precious to me because of memories we shared.'"

Mrs. Gwendolyn K. shared, "Upon his death, I immediately opened his extensive library to several seminary students. Another preacher, a relative, selected several boxes of books to take home to his library. The clergy robes that 'Pastor' owned were given to a minister who asked if it was okay to share them with others. Our son selected [and kept various items of his father's clothing while] the remaining clothes were donated to various charitable organizations."

There is a value in keeping [certain] possessions. In the words of Thomas A. Dorsey, gospel songwriter, "Precious memories, how they linger ..." Also, the significance of remembering, points to the celebration of the Lord's Supper: 'As often as you do this, do it in remembrance of me.' What a precious memory to remember our Lord's love and sacrifice for His believers. So, it is with remembering deceased loved ones.

Each widow wanted to hold on to articles that reminded her of the things they shared in life with their husbands. The items were tangible means of staying connected.

The triadic deaths' impact upon the Haskins clergy family demonstrates not only the emotional consequences but serve as contributory factors militating against the physical health of family members. The participation in grief counseling is strongly recommended by Dr. Haskins, a licensed counselor-educator.

MY INTERVIEW WITH THE REV. DR. JOHN WARREN

Kathleen O'Hara described in her book, titled *A Grief Like No Other: Surviving the Violent Death of Someone You Love,* the experience of receiving a telephone call from the police who notified her of the murder of her son. O'Hara, a therapist, who counseled many others, encountered her worse unimaginable nightmare when she learned of the brutal death of her college-age son, Aaron.

As defined in her book, violent death includes suicide, drug overdose, vehicular homicide, and drunk drivers. Further, she described the nature of violence as unexpected, unpredictable, chaotic and most of all, horrifying. Moreover, violence can occur at any time, at any place, and to anyone. She offered practical and compassionate steps to grieving loved ones. With that in mind, I refer to the experience of a colleague and friend of mine when he encountered his worse unimaginable nightmare. The tragic situation involved his adult son, who lived in Florida, and his young grandson.

The Reverend Doctor John Warren, a retired elder in the United Methodist Church and I are acquaintances dating back to our seminary days at the Howard University, School of Religion, during the mid-1970s. John served, after graduation, a congregation in Martinsburg, West Virginia. We did not reconnect until the early 1990s when I began serving Mount Zion UMC in Baltimore, MD. John served there from 1982 until 1988. From that time on, periodically, we did pulpit exchanges while he served Simpson-Hamlin UMC in Washington, DC., until his appointment to another congregation. Our meetings with one another over the years were incidental to clergy gatherings and annual conferences during which our exchanges were pleasantries, reports about our respective congregations, and the challenges of ministry.

While writing this book, I was uncertain as to how to approach the subject-matter of the unthinkable and painful ordeal of his son and grandson's murder-suicide in 2020 in Naples, Florida. I decided with the utmost of gentleness, rather than to hand him a hardcopy questionnaire or lob determined questions during a telephone interview. Our conversation took on a more personal tone. Honored that he was willing to go *there* with me, I inquired, "John, can I ask you about the tragic incident of the deaths of your son and grandson? As you know," I interjected, "I lost my son four years ago." Immediately, his concern was for me.

He asked, "How are you doing, George?"

I responded, "I have my moments."

After pausing for a moment to let the commonalities of our grief settle in their respective realities, he began to share details about the relationship between him and his son,

Paul, when he was notified about the deaths—and the response of his son's bereaved girlfriend who was the mother of the deceased child, age five.

Surprisingly, my clergy colleague was open, and in some cases, he seemed matter of fact about some of the details. Perhaps his delivery was a defense mechanism.

Rev. Warren served the Brookfield-Immanuel Charge, UMC in Brandywine, MD from July 2018 to July 2021. The congregation viewed itself as, "one congregation at two locations." The Charge is predominantly White, a "cross-over appointment" for Rev. Warren, that is to say, an African American pastor serving a White congregation. The average attendance for the combined churches is eighty members, twice a month. The Charge serves the nearby communities of Baden and Croom in Prince George's County, MD; both are unincorporated communities and census-designated places. Croom is situated three miles north of Brookfield, while Baden is located four miles southwest of the Charge. During John's pastorate at this Charge, he learned of the horrific situation in Naples, Florida.

My colleague shared with me the following: "I received a call from the police and medical examiners from Florida on February 10, 2020. They told me that my son, Paul, was dead from a self-inflicted gunshot wound. My grandson, Colton, was also found dead. Both bodies were in the apartment in East Naples, Florida. The gun was found in Paul's hand."

To say the least, it was an unthinkable and absolute trauma, as the pastor became aware of the details of this tragedy.

Rev. Warren upon hearing this devastating news immediately went into shock, winding up in the fellowship hall of the church where some of the ladies of the church were meeting. He was bereft and openly wept aloud as he told them of the deaths of his son and grandson. The ladies consoled him as much as possible until such time he was able to drive home to be with his wife with whom he sought comfort.

At some point later, Rev. Warren called his deceased son's girlfriend, the mother of the deceased five-year-old son. The child's mother was livid. During the call, the angry bereft mother leveled, "I don't give a [expletive] what you do with [Paul's] body!" The call abruptly ended.

Paul's body was transported back to Maryland. The members of Brookfield UMC, out of compassion and kindness, allowed the body of the pastor's son to be buried in the church's new cemetery.

John reflected on the death of his forty-five-year-old son, his disclosed episodes of depression from his young adult life onward. There was even a period when there was a five-year communication gap between father and son—after Paul attended the University of Miami and continued to reside in Florida. On the occasions during which John met with his son, those meetings were not harmonious. The pastor expressed regret concerning his relationship with Paul.

Grief counseling from Rev. Warren's perspective is positive, with some reservations. The pastor learned from his divorce, many years ago, that counseling helps when dealing with painful circumstances. But issues concerning mental health, and particularly grief counseling, according to Rev. Warren, should not be viewed as a stigma. However, John elaborated further, that if he were to seek out counseling, he would be reluctant to receive grief counseling from colleagues within the denomination. The possibility of confidential matters discussed in grief counseling would seep-out; as a result, was his summation. Instead, he sought grief counseling from friends and professional individuals who were not connected with the Baltimore-Washington Conference, the United Methodist Church. John did not elucidate further reasons for his lack of confidence in counselors connected with the UMC.

The details pertinent to the funeral services for Paul neither entered our fragile conversation nor did I push for such information, keeping in mind the painfully delicate recollection of the murder-suicide. John averred, however, that he sought counseling from a Rev. Clark Aist, former director of Clinical Pastoral Counseling (CPE) and friend. At the time of his counseling of Rev. Warren, Rev. Aist was the Director of Protestant Chapel Activities at St. Elizabeth's Hospital, Washington, DC. Rev. Warren felt that the time with Rev. Aist was quite helpful and meaningful. Also, there were clergy friends in the Episcopal church, he confided in concerning aspects of his grief. Again, using his phrasing, my colleague's apparent concern was for personal information, "creeping back into," the BWC UMC, thus stigmatizing him as a pastor with mental-health issues and in need of grief counseling.

There are spiritual experiences that occur which help bereaved persons have a connection with their loved ones. Such an event, I believed happened to both John and I. John said, "I had a dream that Paul came to me and said, 'I am sorry, Dad'." It was at that point when the Rev. Warren felt a sense of relief in his grief. He opined that Paul was sorry for the trouble he caused in their lives. I also shared an experience in which I felt my late son's presence. Christopher came to me during a time of my devotions. I heard him say, "I'm okay, Dad." Both of us felt that those experiences helped us to progress in our grief. However, I am aware that some reading this may think that we are crazy.

O'Hara wrote in her book, "Many, during their grief, feel they have 'crazy' feelings and thoughts ...This is something not often spoke about in our culture, yet it is a natural, strong part of grief. In fact, denying it only makes it worse..." Also, O'Hara stated, "It takes time to adjust to such profound and sudden absence, to be able to let go of the person's presence within your perception of your immediate world. Whenever you wonder if you have lost your mind, remind yourself: you have lost someone you love, not your mind."

I feel the experiences we had were beneficial and we should not perceive ourselves as being crazy.

OBSERVATIONS

The Reverend Doctor John Warren is a retired clergy member of the Baltimore-Washington Conference, The United Methodist Church. He served two congregations in the Washington East District prior to his retirement. Rev. Dr. Warren disclosed that he received counseling from a former United Methodist pastor after an unsuccessful first marriage many years ago. He attributes the success of his current marriage to that prior counseling. He and his present wife are happily married and have a daughter who recently graduated from the University of Maryland.

Primarily nurtured in the former Methodist Episcopal Church, now the United Methodist Church, Rev. Dr. Warren began his pastoral career on July 1, 1980, at Mount Zion UMC, Martinsburg, West Virginia, and in subsequent years served various congregations as an active pastor in the Baltimore-Washington Conference, UMC. He retired on June 30, 2021; on January 2, 2022, he accepted a role as an interim pastor serving Lanham UMC, Lanham, MD. On July 1, 2022, he began serving the Saint Matthews UMC in Shadyside, MD.

The phone interviews conducted with Rev. Dr. Warren can be described as open, although there was no *push* for horrid details about the tragic murder-suicide of his grandson and son. Yet, he volunteered the information that a gun was used. Occasionally, the pastor interjected comments of happier times, but his focus was on situations that created a gulf in his relationship with his deceased son.

The complicated relationship and deaths constitute a painful sorrow that still lingers with him. As a result, he expresses a staunch anti-gun attitude—the current zeitgeist.

Rev. Dr. Warren served four predominantly White congregations during his extensive pastoral career and was faithful to the ministries of the said churches. At the time of the tragic deaths of his son and grandson, the parishioners of Brookfield-Immanuel UMC, where he was serving at the time, were extremely compassionate and supportive of his immediate family. The church offered burial space for his deceased son.

Rev. Dr. Warren is a firm supporter of counseling for clergy, and that's why he sought marriage counseling from a United Methodist chaplain. However, when it came to confronting his grief due to the loss of his son and grandson, and the perceived salacious circumstances surrounding those deaths, Pastor Warren divulged and overriding concern that the matter of confidentiality could fracture and seep to clergy supervisors, resulting in the fear of losing out on future career opportunities. Moreover, he was not confident that all colleagues would maintain discretion. John sought grief counseling from clergy friends in the Episcopalian community of faith.

Contra to the image of clergy that presents the persona of spiritually strong faith-leaders with a biblical and theological insularity pertinent to grief, overall, Rev. Dr. John Warren favored taking advantage of grief counseling or therapy. His example offers hope and insight to ministers who may be undecided whether to choose to walk the journey of grief and mourning alone or have a guide to assist them. That said, Pastor Warren acknowledges that there are still pastors who opt to remain faithful to the traditional approach of taking it to the Lord in prayer.

CHAPTER SEVEN

Recognizing, Respecting and Releasing Bereaved Robes

Grief counseling was the significant help I needed to open my robe and confront my personal grief, a gripping pain and immobilizing power, that I suppressed and hid under the veil of being a strong pastor unaffected by the emotional spill of the deaths of my family members, as evidenced in several episodes of my life. My mother died in 1990, when I was in my first appointment as a pastor in the Baltimore-Washington Conference of the United Methodist Church. As a recapitulation from Chapter One, *The Painful Memory Episodes*, I suppressed my feelings of grief until two weeks later after my mother's burial. I experienced a meltdown in the privacy of my home office. At that time in my ministry, I did not want anyone to see me—the pastor—in a state of emotional distress. Gregory P. Wynot reported in *The Wall Street Journal*, 2003, the comment of one priest. "...You have to appear confident ... No one wants to see their pastor weeping uncontrollably." My thinking at the time was similar. I did not seek grief counseling based on the erroneous assumption that a pastor should be spiritually invincible; therefore, I felt it was not a problem for me to handle my grief—alone. Hence, it was best for me to maintain a professional distance and refrain from sharing my troubles with the parishioners of the Saint Marks UMC congregation.

Also, I put up a façade of spiritual strength to cover-up my true feelings. As I have said, *I stuffed my feelings inside my robe* to continue on with ministry as usual. Even in the presence of colleagues, I maintained the same demeanor.

Nearly three decades later, I found myself in the painful circumstances of my adult son, Christopher's death, who died of renal failure. I still re-live that dark night and early morning as my son transitioned. Moments following his decease, I was very transparent with my emotions, in Room 6, where my son's lifeless body laid on the hospital bed with all the attached devices and monitors on his body—now silent. Chris' mother and my former wife, Jean, urged me to leave the room to allow the nurses to detach him from the life-support equipment. To use her words, she gently spoke, "Come on, Franklin, let them clean up his body." She called me by my middle name.

We left the room and entered the outer family waiting room where there could be heard, the sympathetic murmurs of various family members and friends, standing and hugging each other in several intimate clusters. It was a surreal setting at 4:30 a.m.

The attending nurse called us to come to the room after Chris' body was cleaned. While I cannot remember how many of us assembled around my son's bed, Travia, my niece, asked, "Can we recite the 23rd Psalm?" Allowing her to lead, we all joined in the recitation.

Next, I placed my hand on my son's forehead and muttered a prayer, ending with, "The Lord giveth, the Lord taketh away. Blessed be the name of the Lord."

The following days were a conglomeration of attending the annual conference in Baltimore City at the Marriott Inner Harbor Hotel. A business meeting with the funeral director at Vaugh C. Greene Funeral Home in Randallstown and securing funds from my credit union in Crofton to take care of the funeral expenses, interrupted. Moreover, I had committed myself to be present at the certification service of two members of Smith Chapel UMC; the certification service was the first order of business with the Board of Ordained Ministry.

The Lay ministers from Smith Chapel UMC were Jocelyn R. and Perry Taylor. I felt I needed and wanted to support them during this special occasion during their journey in ministry. At the conclusion of the ceremony, I greeted them and took pictures with these newly certified ministers of my congregation. After the celebration moments, I returned to my hotel room to get Lila, my wife. We needed to head to the Vaughn C. Greene Funeral Chapel to meet with the funeral representative assisting with the preparations for my son's service.

Ellen, now my son's widow, was too grieved to participate in the business matters of Chris' funeral. Although Jean, my ex-wife and Chris' mother, stretched to share in the arrangements. Quite honestly, I mentally shifted into the busy-pastor mode. In hindsight, I can say that it was an out-of-body experience. Chapter One details the full activities of the Celebration of Life service for Christopher.

What is significant of this retelling of the loss of my son is that after Chris' funeral service, I did not seek help to address my ravaging grief. In fact, the notion to reach out for help never even crossed my heavily burdened mind. Instead, what materialized was a façade. I projected, or so I thought, a seasoned pastor capable of managing his grief in the presence of colleagues, friends, and members of his congregation. After thirty-seven years in ministry, the role of clergy was second nature to me. However, in this moment of harrowing emotional pain, the truth was that I needed the professional help of a grief therapist. Moreover, it was obvious to others around me, such as Mrs. Karleen, P., my co-member of the Morgan State University, Southern Maryland Alumni Chapter. Mrs. P. is also a retired music teacher, guidance counselor and widow who suffered a prolonged period of grief. She readily discerned my dilemma. She emphatically said, "Reverend DeFord, you need help."

To many—and I will never know just how many—my façade was thinly veiled. I was in desperate need of counseling. I believe that in moments of personal grief, when—or if—a clergyperson can come to the reality that to self-manage their suffering may not be beneficial, but instead, acknowledge their need for the professional help of a grief counselor or therapist—bereaved robes will become less burdened.

Nevertheless, in view of my emotional predicament, I sought out and finally registered for grief counseling with the Hospice of Charles County, and began January 18, 2019, at 11 a.m. with Ms. Hayley Bacon, a Licensed Master Social Worker (LMSW) Counselor and Bereavement Coordinator. The Hospice of Charles County, Inc., in Waldorf, MD, is a facility that provides hospice, palliative, and grief care for patients and families. As part of the agency's program, it eases the journey of patients and guides people to cope with their grief. Ms. Bacon counseled me for ten sessions.

For the next remaining nine weeks, appointments began between 9 and 11 a.m. Lasting an hour, they hardly ever stretched beyond the appointed scheduled time. We met in a quiet room with a sign on the door that read *In Session*. Rare-to-nonexistent did disturbances reign. For some reason, I took note of that.

Our initial session began with an interview and the reason for my seeking help. Ms. Bacon began the session inquiring about how I was feeling. She asked how were things going in my life? She quietly and skillfully led me into the issue of the day. She allowed me the freedom to open up about what troubled me—minus the self-induced burden of coming up with any conclusive answers for it all. And nor did she offer any. At the conclusion of that first session, we scheduled the next meeting.

My time with Ms. Bacon concluded on March 15, 2019. She extended the invitation to check in periodically. In addition to that, she said, "whenever there is an annual group meeting with former clients," that I could join. I did not follow up with those offers. Honestly, I regret not continuing with the counseling, blaming it on my presumed busy schedule mandated by the business of the church. However, my reluctance to share my grief experience with others not in the craft halted me as well.

Two sessions remain vivid in my mind. The first occasion occurred when I recalled an incident when Chris was in the sixth grade. I'd had a meeting with his homeroom teacher, who informed me of my son's playing with toy soldiers with another pupil. Chris had been warned about his behavior but did not refrain from his play. And that's what sent me to the school. The teacher took me to Chris' locker that was cluttered with comic books and toy soldiers. In the heat of the moment, I made him take all the clutter out of his locker and throw it into a trashcan. His eyes watered and tears streamed down his face, while he threw away the miniature soldiers and comic books. His teacher said nothing. We left the school, and I scolded him on the way home, emphatically telling him that he would not disobey the teacher or me again. Once at home, I whipped Chris for his disobedience.

Whatever triggered that memory caused me to break down like a child. The counselor left the room until such time I recomposed myself to continue on with the session.

The counselor at the end of the session asked me to write an imaginary letter from Chris for the next session. "What would Chris say to you in this letter?" she asked.

In preparation for next week's session, I continued to replay in my mind the time I made Chris throw away his toy soldiers and comic books. Moreover, I remember that while preparing for his funeral, decades later, when I found myself standing in my son's home office. There was a ledge on the upper wall garnished with superhero figurines. Toy soldiers stood guard along the ledge over the door seal. Chris had his toy soldiers, again, and out of the reach of his father! I wrote the imaginary letter, but I did not mention the comic books or toy soldiers reacquired.

Perhaps, now, as I write freely about his treasured toys, bringing forth into the light that entire incident—it is therapeutic. And what did I imagine my son would have said? "Dad, there is one thing I wished you would have done. Couldn't you have more often said, 'I love you, Chris?'" I'd like to think that Chris would have forgiven me for forcing him to throw away his treasures.

Overall, I think that such an act of imaginary questioning touched the essence of my inner-feelings of guilt and neglect over not paying more attention to my child, but instead putting the busyness of churchwork before him—and the rest of the family.

At the next session, I shared my letter with the counselor. Again, I felt as if another crying spell was about to occur; I went silent for a while. The conversation resumed, but it is difficult for me to recall the further details of the matter. In retrospect, writing the imaginary letter had a cathodic effect of releasing some of my pent-up feelings.

We met until the tenth session during which time there was a recapitulation of our meetings. As mentioned earlier, Ms. Bacon had left open the opportunity for me to return and/or meet with a group of former clients. And even as more years have passed, while I did not take advantage of her offered periodic check-ins, because the initial sessions were beneficial, reflectively, I wish I had.

The benefit I received from the grief counseling/therapy helped me to open my *bereaved robe persona* and address issues I suppressed. The counseling helped me to understand the way I dealt with my pain. The revelation that surfaced was pointed to a longstanding issue in my life as it related to my deceased son. I wanted to be his rescuer! From Chris' infancy to his adult life, he experienced medical problems. I attempted to save him from various problems throughout. I shared episodes in my son's life during certain sessions.

Chris at the age of two years old, suffered from cancer of his right eye. As a desperate and concerned father, I took him to several ophthalmologists and oncologists, seeking to save his eye. After exhausting all medical resources, I finally came to the conclusion as did his mother, my former wife, that our child's right eye had to undergo ocular surgery, a procedure known as enucleation—the surgical removal of the entire eyeball with the lining of the eyelid and muscles of the eye. Before the final decision, I asked one ophthalmologist could my eye be given to him as a transplant? The physician informed me that only the pupil of the eye could be transplanted and his situation was beyond that. I was devastated.

My son's surgery was at the Wilmer Eye Clinic Johns Hopkins Hospital in Baltimore City. What stands out in my mind was when his mother brought him home. Etched in my memory is Chris looking up with the gaping red cavernous opening on the right side of his little swollen face while holding his Curious George monkey in his right arm. His toy monkey had a medical patch over its right eye. I lost it! I literally screamed, "Oh no!" as I fell to my knees in the dining room. "Why did God let this happen? It's not fair!"

His mother, feeling forced to come to the defense of our son, more than to comfort me, said," Franklin, don't scare him!" Crying, I went downstairs to the family-recreation room where I went to the bar, grab some whiskey, and began drinking from the bottle at the same time profusely crying. I hoped the liquor would soothe the pain I was feeling. I could not protect, rescue or save my son!

The next episode was my son's completing his education. For much of Chris' life, he shuttled between his mother's home in Baltimore City and our home, in Prince George's County, Maryland. His mother finally let Lila and I have custody of him. Thinking he would receive a better education in a private school over-and-against public school, we enrolled him in a military academy in New

Bloomfield, Pennsylvania. After two years, Chris' arm was broken as a result of an incident in the local town, I believe it was an issue of racism. Chris nor the school administration gave an explanation as to what happened. He refused to tell my wife and I what happened. At that point, we dis-enrolled him from the military school and enrolled him in Surratt's High School in Clinton, MD. My feeling at that time was I did not adequately protect my son.

High school was a disappointment for us as Chris became a truant by skipping school bus rides in the morning. Finally, in November 1987, he ran away. The Maryland State Police picked him up as he walked northbound on the Capital Beltway in Prince George's County. Rather than call us, the state police contacted his mother, Jean, in Baltimore. She responded to the station where Chris was, took custody of him, came to our house and angrily got his belongings and returned to Baltimore with him. About six months passed before I saw or spoke with him. Finally, with his mother's consent, Chris began visiting with us; we emphasized to him that we would not make him stay and would return him to Jean after his weekend visits.

We discovered Chris' truancy, again, in his senior year of high school in Baltimore. It was clear during one of our weekend visits. Instead of simply returning him to Jean on a Sunday evening, I took him to school that Monday morning. And that's how I found out he had been truant. Right then and there, I decided to force myself back into his daily life. I interceded on his behalf with the principal of the school. I agreed to call the school weekly and driving from Prince George's County, Maryland to Baltimore to attend Parents and Teachers Association meetings. Eventually, teachers reported that Chris made a complete turn-around and would be on track for graduating in June 1990. On hearing the positive information, I encouraged Chris to apply to Morgan State University. He applied for admission, and I was elated. However, my anticipation of his entering my alma mater soon ended when he informed me that he would be moving to Boston, Massachusetts after graduation. He planned to seek employment and teach color guard marching maneuvers with a group of youngsters. I went ballistic!

My son's decision to not attend the university was painful and angered me. This was the emotional baggage I *stuffed inside my robe*, due to my desire to control Christopher's life. I used as a refrain at times, "if you would have gone to college ..."

Lila and I saw Christopher off to Boston and put money in his hand at the airport. His stay there would not last, and he returned to Baltimore, bouncing from one job to another—still needing help from us.

Another example that surfaced during therapy sessions was giving my son money to pay his rent and get provisions for his family the first of September of each year, before receiving his pay, working for a recreation department in Baltimore County, Maryland. Secretly, I confess that I always went back to the matter: *had you gone to college, you wouldn't be in this predicament each year.*

The next major episode was the matter of a kidney transplant. Again, I went to have my kidney transplanted to my son. This was not to be. The result of my evaluation procedure at the University of Maryland Hospital in Baltimore concluded that I was not a viable candidate. My diabetes, hypertension, and obesity constituted the key factors, rendering me helpless to come to Christopher's rescue. In addition, my age militated against the transplant surgery. I was seventy-three years old at the time. Again, I could do nothing to save my son!

The process of the therapy sessions revealed the burdens I unceremoniously, but consistently stowed inside my clergy robe. Subconsciously, I suppose, my robe was not only my coping mechanism, but also my shield. A sense of powerlessness to rescue my son from the clutches of death's icy grip, yielded the ultimate intensities of guilt. I also wrestled with the matter of image; how did I look to my colleagues and parishioners. Finally, I treated Christopher as an invalid who needed protection. He did not!

***

How many others are there—how many others will there be—to walk in my shoes. For clergy, strong in faith and dedicated to service—acknowledging the need of grief counseling should not be synonymous with an appearance of weakness or loss of effectiveness, a threat to one's career or an affront to one's faith in God.

I'm hopeful that in similar circumstances that more clergy will take advantage of grief counseling—without the fear of being stigmatized. Maybe, this is why active clergy avoid taking counseling/therapy unless required by the denominational judicatory. By the same token, I'm hopeful that denominations will be more affirmative of their clergy voluntarily taking the opportunity to receive the benefits of grief counseling. Labelling a pastor who suffers from mental health issues or grief—because unattended grief could trigger mental health struggles—could potentially create a modeling of suppressing emotional issues among congregants. Such would be detrimental.

CHAPTER EIGHT

A Step in the Right Direction

The thrust of this book concerns clergy confronting personal grief due to the deaths of their child(ren). Limited attention focused on the responses of congregations whose pastors suffered the sorrow of losing a loved one. Recently, a group of clergypersons in the Baltimore-Washington Conference of the United Methodist Church (BWCUMC) revealed instances in which congregants expressed insensitivity as their pastors grieved the loss of loved ones. The lack of concern manifested in such ways as failure to grant a sufficient time for clergy bereavement leave to grieve and mourn their loss or chastised the minister for expressing his or her sorrowful feelings. The behavior of the church members perhaps could be attributed to a cultural perception of pastors being above emotional displays of personal sorrow. For example, a senior lady, daughter of a late pastor of many years ago, believed that her father was the paragon of spiritual strength who could not be brought to tears. That kind of thinking was prevalent among the older generation of parishioners and pastors. However, attitudes are changing; the image of bereaved pastors is slowly evolving into one of an acceptance of public shows of emotion.

The Rev. Terri Coffiell, a full member of the BWC UMC shared with the author two instances wherein the lack of concern for her well-being were really painful. Rev. Coffiell's husband died seven years ago. What exacerbated Terri's sorrow was the insensitive treatment she received during the mourning of her husband. According to the pastor, there was a lack of empathy exhibited by the congregants.

Pastor Coffiell's mother transitioned that left her with profound sorrow. While in the pulpit, she said, "I can't handle this anymore. I need help."

After the worship service, an elderly female member chastised her, "You need to get yourself together. You are not supposed to act like that."

In the narthex, Terri sternly retorted, "Listen chick if you have been through what I've been through, you would understand!"

The cases of pastors confronting their personal grief and the varying reactions of the churches triggered a group of United Methodist clergy persons, active and retired, to sponsor a resolution pertinent to the matter of a bereavement protocol and policy. The principles in the protocol serve as an operative solution to assist clergy dealing with the issues of grief and mourning and an appropriate time for healing.

The resolution addresses what pastors need; yet implicit in it is the need for congregations to become more sensitized to and trained in the needs of their clergy. A mandate needs to be implemented for churches to receive further training pertaining to the well-being of their pastors. Specifically, in the United Methodist Church, the Staff Parish Relations Committee (SPRC) should be trained. Such formal training could be beneficial for other communities of faith.

Melissa Lauber, Director of Communications, Baltimore-Washington Conference, The United Methodist Church, authorized the presentation of the resolution in part:

Title: Establishment of a BWC Clergy Bereavement Protocol and Policy

Budget Implications: There are no Conference budget implications.

Rationale: Surviving the death of a spouse or child requires the reordering of every aspect of life; this is true for clergy as well as laypersons. Since few pastors are adequately trained in processing grief, it is unrealistic to expect a congregation to understand or address the needs of a bereaved pastor. While not attempting to cover every situation regarding the death of a loved one, the following resolution establishes precedent and sets a baseline for response, providing much-needed direction to congregations seeking to support their pastors at critical life moments.

Submitted by: Terri Cofiell...Elder in Full Connection

RESOLUTION:

Whereas there is no existing policy specifically regarding clergy bereavement leave in the Baltimore-Washington Conference Policy and Procedure Manual;

Whereas the death of a spouse or child is among the most traumatic life events a person can experience; and whereas unresolved grief can impact the physical and mental health of even the most devout people of faith;

Whereas clergy of often sacrifice self-care and family relationships in order to meet the needs and demands of their parishioners; and where the compassionate care of grief-stricken pastors has been left solely to congregations to offer (or withhold); now

Therefore, be it

Resolved, that The Baltimore-Washington Conference of The United Methodist Church adopt the following protocol and policy regarding bereavement leave for all Full and part-time ordained clergy and licensed pastors under appointment within the bounds of the Conference.

. Within 48 hours after notification of the death of a clergy's spouse, child, or parent, the District Superintendent shall collaborate with the SPRC to arrange pastoral coverage for the charge including, but not limited to, worship planning, preaching, pastoral care, and any immediate administrative needs.

. The Superintendent will emphasize to the SPRC the need of the pastor for space and time to grieve and help the committee to discern appropriate ways to offer care and support. It will be stressed that pressing parish needs be addressed to the District Administrator until the pastor returns from leave.

. The Superintendent, in conjunction with the District Administrator, shall provide to the SPRC a list of potential supply ministers, Certified Lay Speakers/Ministers, as well as retired and neighboring clergy. In addition, the Superintendent will inform (via email) possible supply/neighboring/retired pastors of the impending need.

. The pastor's Full salary shall be maintained for six to eight weeks following the death of a spouse or child, and one to two weeks following the death of a parent. The length of the bereavement leave will be determined through consultation between the pastor and Superintendent.

. Bereavement leave will be in addition to and not subtracted from vacation time, continuing education time, and/or days off. The local church or conference agency to which the clergy is appointed shall continue to provide salary and housing as well as pension and insurance payment, during the Full bereavement leave period.

Effective Date: July 1, 2023

Co-Sponsors: Twenty-eight clergypersons were the signatories of active and retired Full Elders statuses.

***

The clergy and lay members of the Baltimore-Washington Conference of The United Methodist Church overwhelmingly voted to enact the resolution to become official policy on July 1, 2023. In view of this action, hope abounds.

A Dark Moment for God // But A Resurrection of Hope

Grief and mourning are parts of the human condition. For clarity, grief is the internal experience of profound sorrow. Mourning is the external manifestation of that feeling. Down through the generations, the manifestation of mourning takes place in a variety of cultural ways.

The Bible reveals several narratives pertinent to biblical characters who experienced the death of their loved ones and how they grieved and mourned. Job, the patriarch in biblical antiquity, is an example of one who grieved the loss of his children by following the ritual of mourning. Job tore his robe, shaved his head, and fell on the ground and worshipped. He said, "Naked I came from my mother's womb, and naked shall I return there; the Lord gave, and the Lord has taken away; blessed be the name of the Lord" (Job 1:20, 21). As it was with Job, so it is with us, we encounter grief that death causes and respond in some form of mourning, regardless of the culture.

Grief lingers as an entombment. The person who grieves experiences a sense of captivity and darkness without a means of deliverance. Yet, Jesus Christ who is our redeemer, who was entombed in a borrowed tomb, from Friday night until the early hours of the first day of the week; so is clergy grief that is suppressed in the metaphorical robes. But there is the promise of resurrection that gives hope. No longer must grief be carried inside the minister's robes. With Christian counseling/therapy, renewed life comes. It's faith and hope that is resident within the clergy person that promises new life through the power of Almighty God.

Good Friday, in the Christian community is the occasion to commemorate the death of Jesus the Son of God. For African American churches, The Seven Last Words services are typically conducted from 12 noon to 3 p.m. In many cases, the speakers' rousing proclamations cause both preachers and congregants to come to their feet in praise. The significance of the *hour* focuses upon our Lord and His redemptive act of death upon the cross as payment for our salvation. Yet, I wonder how many attendees and worshipers reflect upon the divine grief that Abba suffered while God's only begotten Son endured the excruciating pain from the lacerated wounds on His back and the George Floyd-like suffocation while hanging from the cross beam, until succumbing to death on the old rugged cross? The sacrificial death of our Lord was prefigured by Abraham preparing to sacrifice his son Isaac (Genesis 22:6—11). I imagine Abraham pondered over the anticipatory grief that would result from his obedience to God to sacrifice his son, Isaac, on a woodpile. Further, Jesus, the Son of God, weeping at Lazarus' tomb is another example of grieving but with the unique twist with Immanuel (God with us), weeping openly in the presence of people. In their affliction, God was afflicted.

The emotional pain of a parent losing a child is not new. Koheleth, the Preacher, candidly reminds the reader that the thing which has been is the same that will be, succinctly, "... there is nothing new under the sun" (Ecclesiastes 1:9). Grief is a part of the human condition.

Throughout the Bible, episodes of biblical characters suffering the emotional pain of sorrow for the loss of a beloved one, especially a child, is well documented in both the Hebrew Scriptures and the New Testament.

Another side of the issue of grief is God's grief associated with the transgressions of humankind. The account of godly sorrow cited in Genesis shows the grief God felt and the choice made to ameliorate the problem (Genesis 6:5–7). Judgment came upon humanity in the form of a horrendous deadly flood. The manifestation of God's grief began, "... In the six hundredth year of Noah's life, in the second month, on the seventh day of the month, on that day all the fountains of the great deep burst forth, and the windows of the heavens were opened" (Genesis 7:11). That fatal event in Noah's life was the day God openly showed God's grief and mourning. Hence, God's grief was implicit in God's judgment, but not hindering.

The Synoptic Gospels, Matthew, Mark and Luke, describe without significant variation the darkness that occurred during Jesus' crucifixion. Luke says, "It was now about noon, and darkness came over the whole land until three in the afternoon," (Luke 23:44). Darkness in the biblical context brings to mind several meanings: ignorance of God, sin, sorrow, judgment, grief, and death. With attention to the period of darkness on that fateful day, Good Friday afternoon, Jesus' crucifixion points to God's displeasure, grief, and judgment against Jewish religionists, their followers, and gentiles. While Jesus, the sacrificial Lamb of God, moaned and uttered psalms from His lips while hanging from the cross, God remained silent. Yet, the darkness over the land showed God's righteous anger and judgment against a recalcitrant people. God, the Father, in the cosmic order displayed godly grief by causing darkness over the land. Also, there was the fulfillment of the oracle of Amos, the Tekoan shepherd from the southern kingdom, who said, "On that day, says the Lord God, I will make the sun go down at noon, and darken the earth in broad daylight...I will make it like the mourning for an only son, and the end of it like a bitter day," (Amos 8:9, 10). This was a dark moment for God as God grieved and mourned.

Again, I offer some thoughts on the matter of clergy struggling with the dilemma of personal grief. Respectfully, I refer to that as *clergy grief.*

The Creator's Moments of Divine Grief

The dark shadow cast over the land while Jesus was dying on the cross was an incomprehensible cosmic occurrence. The darkness was not an obscuration of the sun by the moon that would last for a few moments; instead, it was the divine sign and the fulfillment of prophecy as spoken by the prophet Amos: "... I will make the sun go down at noon ..." (Amos 8: 9).

In *John Gill's Exposition of the Entire Bible,* the commentator cites regarding the darkness over the land: "...Heathen historians and chronologers, as Phlegon, and others, referred to by Eusebius (d) The Roman archives are appealed unto for the truth of it by Tertullian (e); and it is asserted by Surdas, that Dionysius the Areopagite...saw it in Egypt and said, 'either the divine being suffers, or suffers with him that suffers, or the frame of the world is dissolving'

"Another translation says, '...either the God of nature is suffering or either the machinery of the world is being dissolved.'"

God's role as Creator and Divine Parent did not immune God from feeling the devastating loss as a parent. The obscuration of daylight in the natural order signified the Divine Parent's sorrow yet the necessary sacrifice of His child for the redemption of humankind. For the three hours of the Son's suffering and dying on the cross on Golgotha Hill, the Creator grieved too while judging humankind. This happened during God's darkest moment of grieving and mourning.

In light of the foregoing, I submit clergy are not immune from the pains of grief and can express their mourning openly while such does not militate against their depth of faith nor spiritual strength. Those of us in the craft of professional ministry have feelings like others who struggle with the deaths of loved ones, especially children. It is not shameful to express one's grief openly while not negating faith in the God whom we serve.

Clergy Challenges, while Confronting Personal Grief

The sampling of the diverse group of clergy and family in my observation presents an area that begs for study. I gathered from my diverse group of clerics that while the younger ministers willingly sought help from grief counselors, the older pastors relied solely upon their faith in God through prayer. And the more senior pastors did so without hesitating to recommend the utilization of grief counselors to bereaved members of their congregations.

Each cleric alluded to the memory of the death of their loved one remaining with them and the ensuing sorrow. Grief is described as a relentless presence staying with them, although at times seemingly to leave them for a while only to return with a vengeance. The haunting recurrences are likened to what C. S. Lewis recounted in his book *A Grief Observed* as a bomber circling prepared to unload its lethal bombs. Others saw grief as an ebb tide that returns unexpectedly or as an unwanted guest, intruder, and last but not least a monster in the closet.

Maintaining the image of a spiritually strong pastor was a significant point. Although not verbalized, the guarded concern was image. Some of the pastors felt as did some of their family members that ministers should not display open sorrow or emotional mourning; such an exhibition could be imputed as a failure to keep the traditional image of a spiritually strong minister—the persona must be maintained. The challenge is being transparent with oneself and his or her congregation.

Career opportunities, some believed, could be jeopardized because of his or her inability to manage personal grief pains, such behavior could be construed as an indication of weakness and ineffectiveness. As a result, they *stuffed their feelings inside their robes* and continued on with ministry as usual. The challenge is not to suppress one's emotional pains under the guise of well-being.

Also, the reputation of a clergyperson among colleagues was a concern. One pastor implied that collegiality could not be trusted when dealing with personal pain. The cleric asserted their reluctance to share with other colleagues in the denomination about their personal grief struggles. Moreover, keeping confidentiality was a high priority because of the fear of information getting back to the judicatory.

The challenge is to prayerfully consult with members of the judicatory to share one's struggle with matters of grief.

The clergy challenges I gleaned from the small group of cohorts were:

A fear to display mourning, openly,

matter of transparency with self and congregation,

the shattering of the traditional pastoral image (e.g., a pastor being overwhelmed in tears), career opportunities possibly jeopardized because of the apparent inability to navigate mental health complications,

and perceived lack of confidentiality among fellow clergy and the judicatory.

Clergy grandparents and extended family members who are clergy, particularly, experienced a similar weight of grief as did the bereft parents. A clergywoman along with her bereaved sister sought help while a clergy grandparent did not. Grief counseling is beneficial for grieving grandparents and extended family members, too.

Clergy are expected to exemplify the presence of Christ for others in their times of weakness. Individually, they are expected to be the faithful disciple of Jesus Christ—steadfast.

The challenge for clergy struggling with the recurrence of grief, seeking help to understand that grief, and learning how to productively deal with the sorrowful feelings of personal grief does not negate a clergyperson's faith in Jesus Christ. Rather the challenges motivate clergypersons to use alternative ways.

Confronting Personal Grief by Way of Divine Positioning Systems

There is a plethora of scriptures pertaining to advice, counsel and hope in both the Hebrew Bible and the New Testament, especially good and wise counsel. Several cases give glimpses of good and bad counsels. In 2 Samuel 16—17, there is a contrast of good and bad counsels exemplified by

Ahitopthel and Hushai who advised Absalom (the son) and King David (the father) respectively, during the son's rebellion. Also in Matthew's gospel, several episodes of counsel to trap and kill Jesus occurred (Matthew 22:15, 27:1; 28:12). The cases show advice that come from those who are not led by godly intent. So, it was leadership, particularly religious leaders in antiquity, that depended upon advice/counsel from those who presumed to speak on behalf of God.

Nathan, the prophet, spoke on behalf of God to David regarding his adulterous affair with Bathsheba. Judgment would come against King David's house, and the child of his affair with Bathsheba, Uriah's wife, would die. Although the king mourned before the child died (anticipatory grief); he ceased the ritual of mourning and went to comfort Bathsheba, who eventually became pregnant again, and Solomon was born (2 Samuel 12:1—25).

God's character is holiness, compassion, and love; although there are occasions when God, begrudgingly and sorrowfully, brings judgment upon a sinful people. In the poetic dirge of Lamentations, the daughter of Zion appealed to God to restore, renew their days of old (5:21—22). Hope still abounds.

***

The death of a child without question evokes profound pain and sorrow that calls for counselors or therapists to assist with the parents struggling with their grief. In the Hebrew Scriptures, the chief priest served as counselor and physician. Leviticus 11—15, served sort as the priest-physician's desk reference. Nowadays, pastoral counselors or faith-based counselors are available to serve members of the communities of faith experiencing the loss of a child(ren). In fact, during the late twentieth century, the academy curricularized pastoral counseling and clinical pastoral education (CPE). One of the resources used was Howard Clinebell's text on basic pastoral counseling. The purpose was to equip seminarians for preparation for ministry in the local church where they could provide basic pastoral counseling. A certain professor during my seminary education contended that a pastor was required to give three counseling sessions and if the issue was not resolved, refer the individual(s) for professional counseling or therapy. It was not the pastor's duty to be a professional counselor or therapist.

Pertinent to the matter of clergy grief, after a pastor conducted a multitude of funerals, such as during the COVID-19 Global Pandemic, to whom does he or she turn to for help with their struggles with personal grief? The sampling of pastors interviewed by this writer dealt with their grief issues by seeking counseling from faith-based counselors or therapists while other chose to seek solutions to their problems through spiritual disciplines of Bible reading and prayer. The said group tended to be older pastors; perhaps the older pastors relied upon the tenets of the psalter: "Trust in him at all times, O people; pour out your heart before him; God is a refuge for us ..." (Psalm 62:8).

Younger pastors were open to seeking help from counselors. A young minister on staff of New Psalmist Baptist Church, Baltimore City, while preaching said, "It's okay to have Christ and a counselor or Jesus and a therapist." Still another pastor in the sampling sought help from colleagues in another denomination. My conclusion is pastors are not of one mindset whether to seek help from counselors or therapists or just primarily rely on their faith in God and spiritual disciplines. It is reasonable to conclude younger clergypersons are more inclined to receive the professional help from counselors and/or therapists than older clergy.

***

Grief counseling was a beneficial experience for me. The process which the counselor guided me through brought to my awareness the hidden issues that needed to be freed from inside my clergy robe and dealt with in healthy ways.

My beloved colleagues there is no harm in being transparent about your feelings of grief and showing the same through outward expressions through mourning! "When the righteous cry for help, the Lord hears, and rescues them from all their troubles. The Lord is near to the brokenhearted and saves the crushed in spirit. Many are the affliction of the righteous, but the Lord rescues them all...," (Psalm 34:17—19). I strongly recommend grief counseling for those who encounter the dark days of the loss of a child, and cry like the ancient king of Israel, "Oh, my [child] my [child]," (2 Samuel 18:33).

The Spirit of God will navigate the clergy seeking help to the grief counselor who can help deal with the personal dilemma of grief.

Grief counseling was a comfort for me to be freed of those suppressed issues that bulged underneath my metaphorical clergy robe. The Greek word for comfort, *parakleseos,* similar to the word for Holy Spirit, *parakletos,* means: to come alongside and help. Jesus in His Sermon on the Mount said, "Blessed are those who mourn, for they will be comforted," (Matthew 5:4). The apostle John gave an answer as to why mourners would be comforted; the apostle declares, "But the Comforter, which is the Holy Ghost, whom the Father will sent in my name, he shall teach you all things, and bring all things to your remembrance, whatsoever I have said unto you," (John 14:26 KJV). Also, the apostle states the sorrow due to Jesus' death will turn to joy as revealed in his comment: "... Very truly, I tell you, you will weep and mourn, but the world will rejoice; you will have pain, but your pain will turn into joy ..." (John 16:20).

As mentioned in the Introduction, grief counselors address the current existential issues affecting a client, while therapists, who deal with grief, focus on helping patients to discover and understand problems originating in their past, impacting their present attitudes and behavior.

So, with the help of a faith-based grief counselor, through whom the Holy Spirit worked, I received comfort, and the understanding of the emotional issues that influenced my mental health state. Just as God experienced a dark moment with the crucifixion of His only begotten Son, so we clergy have our dark moments, too. But the experience can be redemptive and empowering for us to become better servants of God.

About the Author

Rev. Dr. George F. DeFord is a retired full member of the Baltimore-Washington Conference, The United Methodist Church, where he benefits from forty-one years of ordained ministry. He served in various capacities within district and conference areas, significantly as a Regional Guide for the Southern Region. During his post-retirement years, Dr. DeFord was the pastor of Smith Chapel United Methodist Church until contracting COVID-19 in April 2020, which nearly took his life. That near-death pandemic experience caused Rev. Dr. DeFord and his wife, Lila, whom he affectionately calls *My Girlfriend and Wife, who is one and the same* wrote their memoir titled *Miraculous: Pastor and Wife's Account of Illness and Recovery from COVID-19.*

The DeFords make their home in Pomfret, Maryland. Together they have three adult sons, of whom the youngest son deceased in May 2018. They also have two grandsons.